SIDE by SIDE

Extra

Book/eText/ Workbook 1B

Expanded Grammar

Self-Tests & Skill Checks

Digital FunZone & Audio

Steven J. Molinsky • Bill Bliss

Illustrated by Richard E. Hill

Side by Side Extra Book/eText/Workbook 1B

Pearson Education, 10 Bank Street, White Plains, NY 10606

Staff credits: The people who make up the *Side by Side Extra* team, representing content creation, design, manufacturing, marketing, multimedia, project management, publishing, rights management, and testing are Pietro Alongi, Allen Ascher, Rhea Banker, Elizabeth Barker, Lisa Bayrasli, Elizabeth Carlson, Jennifer Castro, Tracey Munz Cataldo, Diane Cipollone, Aerin Csigay, Victoria Denkus, Dave Dickey, Daniel Dwyer, Wanda España, Oliva Fernandez, Warren Fischbach, Pam Fishman, Nancy Flaggman, Patrice Fraccio, Irene Frankel, Aliza Greenblatt, Lester Holmes, Leslie Johnson, Janet Johnston, Caroline Kasterine, Barry Katzen, Ray Keating, Renee Langan, Jaime Lieber, José Antonio Méndez, Julie Molnar, Alison Pei, Pamela Pia, Stuart Radcliffe, Jennifer Raspiller, Kriston Reinmuth, Mary Perrotta Rich, Tania Saiz-Sousa, Katherine Sullivan, Paula Van Ells, Kenneth Volcjak, Paula Williams, and Wendy Wolf.

Contributing authors: Laura English, Megan Ernst, Meredith Westfall

Text composition: TSI Graphics, Inc.

Illustrations: Richard E. Hill

Student book photo credits: Page v (computer) Oleksiy Mark/Fotolia, (tablet on left) Kuzmick/Fotolia, (tablet on right) Can Yesil/Fotolia; p. 98 (top) CandyBox Images/Fotolia, (middle top) Robert Churchill/iStockphoto/Getty Images, (middle bottom) camihesse/Fotolia, (bottom) Image Source/Getty Images; p. 115 WoodyStock/Alamy; p. 116 (top left) Gary Conner/Photodisc/Getty Images, (bottom left) Image Source/Getty Images, (middle) Pixel Embargo/Fotolia, (right) Steve Mason/Photodisc/Getty Images; p. 140 (top) A3528 Armin Weigel Deutsch Presse Agentur/Newscom, (middle) pressmaster/Fotolia, (bottom) IS2 from Image Source/Alamy;
p. 165 (top) Philip Scalia/Alamy, (bottom left) Radharc Images/Alamy, (bottom right) Robert Landau/Alamy; p. 166 (top left) vannphoto/Fotolia, (top middle) Chris Howes/Wild Places Photography/Alamy, (top right) ABW Photography/Purestock/SuperStock, (bottom left) Caro/Alamy, (bottom middle) Ariel Skelley/Blend Images/Getty Images, (bottom right) Patti McConville/Alamy.

The authors gratefully acknowledge the contribution of Tina Carver in the development of the original *Side by Side* program.

ISBN-10: 0-13-245972-8
ISBN-13: 978-0-13-245972-3

Printed in the United States of America
1 2 3 4 5 6 7 8 9 10–V082–23 22 21 20 19 18 17 16

CONTENTS

Introducing the *Side by Side Extra* eText!

The **eText version** of the Student Book offers *instant-access point-of-use audio* and serves as the student's virtual speaking-practice companion. Teachers can "flip" the lesson plan by moving some of the core conversation practice to students' time outside of class, thereby gaining back valuable instruction time for the multilevel expansion activities suggested in the Teacher's Guide, including games, discussion, brainstorming, and role-playing.

Welcome to the **FunZone**—a digital amusement park with attractions for each ***Side by Side Extra*** unit!

Stop by the *Picture Booth* for FlashCards practice and Picture/Word activities. *"Test Your Strength"* at our Vocabulary, Grammar, and Reading challenges. Step right up to the *Game Gallery* to play Concentration, Quiz Show, Crossword, and Lucky Letters games. Visit *ToonTown* for animation-based grammar activities. And don't miss the videos and music at the *ShowTime* stage.

The FunZone is optimized for computers and tablets. Students, BYOD—Bring Your Own Device.

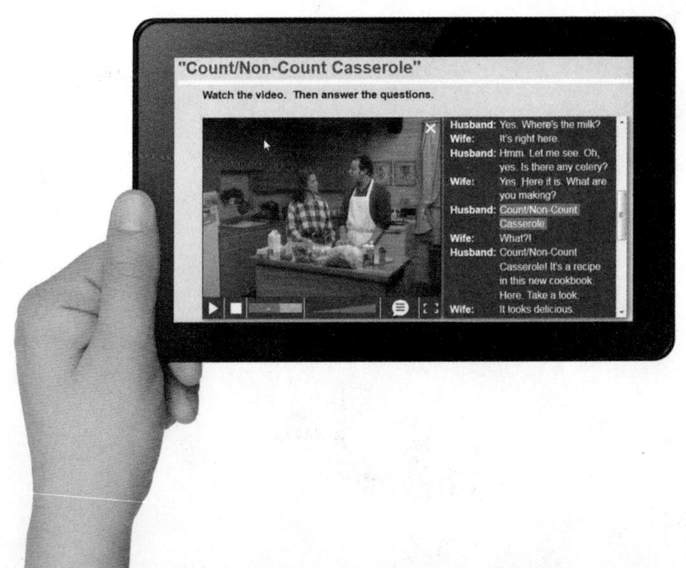

9

Simple Present Tense

- Languages and Nationalities
- Everyday Activities

Vocabulary Preview

1. call
2. cook
3. drive
4. eat
5. listen to music
6. paint
7. play
8. read
9. sell
10. shop
11. sing
12. speak
13. visit
14. watch TV
15. work

Interviews Around the World

I / We / You / They } live.

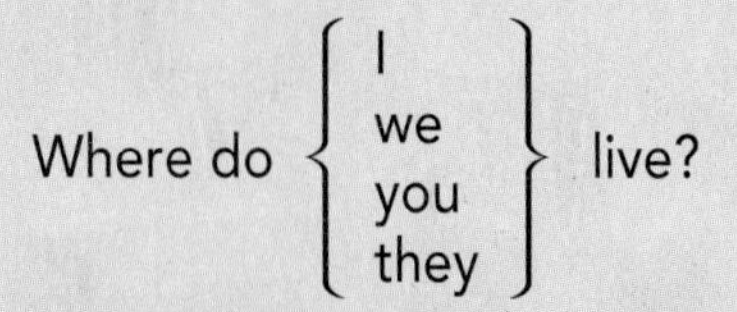

Where do { I / we / you / they } live?

What do { I / we / you / they } do?

A. What's your name?

B. My name is Antonio.

A. Where do you live?

B. I live in Rome.

A. What language do you speak?

B. I speak Italian.

A. Tell me, what do you do every day?

B. I eat Italian food,
I sing Italian songs,
and I watch Italian TV shows!

Interview these people.

What's your name?
Where do you live?
What language do you speak?
What do you do every day?

1.

2.

3.

4.

5. Korean
SEOUL
Jae Hee

6. Russian
MOSCOW
Boris and Natasha

People Around the World

He / She / It } lives.	Where does { he / she / it } live?	What does { he / she / it } do?

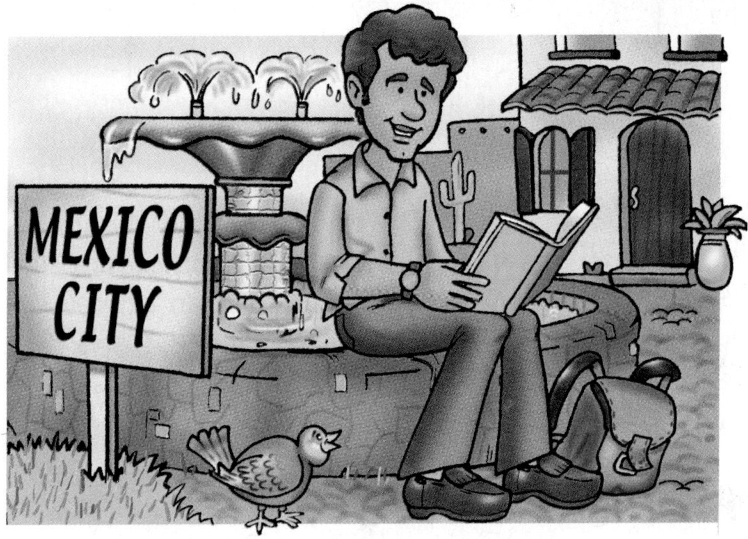

A. What's his name?
B. His name is Miguel.
A. Where does he live?
B. He lives in Mexico City.
A. What language does he speak?
B. He speaks Spanish.
A. What does he do every day?
B. He eats Mexican food,
he reads Mexican newspapers,
and he listens to Mexican music.

Ask and answer questions about these people.

What's his/her name?
Where does he/she live?
What language does he/she speak?
What does he/she do every day?

1. 

2. 

3. 

4. 

5. 

6. 

TALK ABOUT IT! *Where Do They Live, and What Do They Do?*

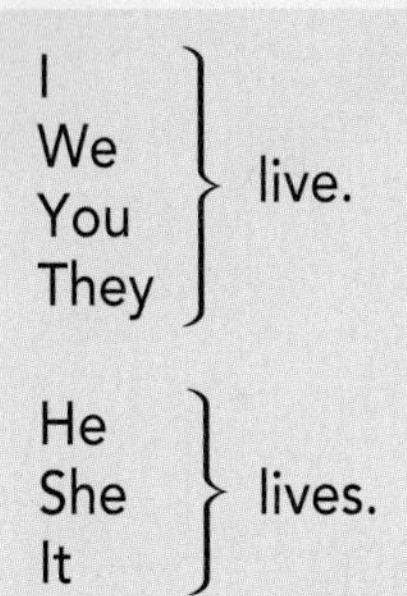

I / We / You / They } live.

He / She / It } lives.

Where { do { I / we / you / they } ; does { he / she / it } } live?

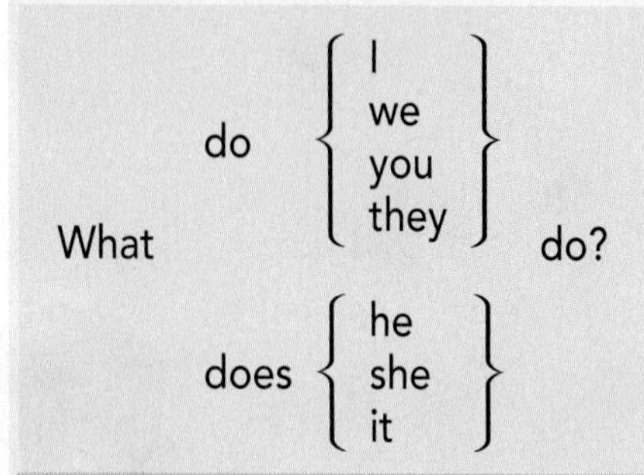

What { do { I / we / you / they } ; does { he / she / it } } do?

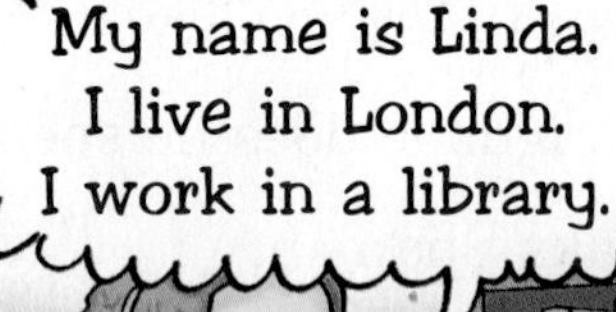

My name is Linda. I live in London. I work in a library.

My name is Brian. I live in Boston. I work in a bank.
We're Walter and Wendy. We live in Washington, D.C. We work in an office.
My name is Bob. I live in Buffalo. I drive a bus.
We're Howard and Henry. We live in Honolulu. We paint houses.

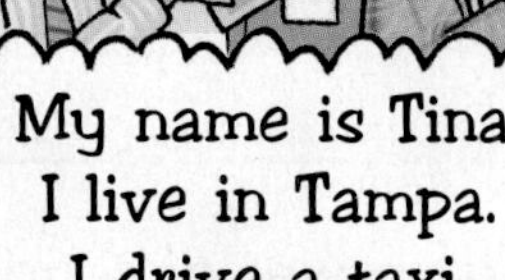

My name is Tina. I live in Tampa. I drive a taxi.

We're Carol and Ray. We live in Cleveland. We cook in a restaurant.
My name is Susan. I live in San Diego. I sell cars.
My name is Victor. I live in Vancouver. I play the violin.

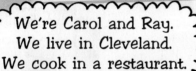

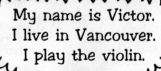

Use these models to talk with other students about the people above.

A. Where does *Linda* live?
B. *She* lives in *London*.
A. What does *she* do?
B. *She works in a library.*

A. Where do *Walter* and *Wendy* live?
B. They live in *Washington, D.C.*
A. What do they do?
B. They *work in an office.*

How About You?

Where do you live? What do you do?

MR. AND MRS. DiCARLO

Mr. and Mrs. DiCarlo live in an old Italian neighborhood in New York City. They speak a little English, but usually they speak Italian.

They read the Italian newspaper. They listen to Italian radio programs. They shop at the Italian grocery store around the corner from their apartment building. And every day they visit their friends and neighbors and talk about life back in "the old country."

Mr. and Mrs. DiCarlo are upset about their son, Joe. He lives in a small suburb outside the city. He speaks a little Italian, but usually he speaks English. He reads American newspapers. He listens to American radio programs. He shops at big suburban supermarkets and shopping malls. And when he visits his friends and neighbors, he always speaks English.

In fact, Joe speaks Italian only when he calls his parents on the telephone, or when he visits them every weekend.

Mr. and Mrs. DiCarlo are sad because their son speaks so little Italian. They're afraid he's forgetting his language, his culture, and his country.

✓ READING *CHECK-UP*

WHAT'S THE ANSWER?

1. Where do Mr. and Mrs. DiCarlo live?
2. Where does Joe live?
3. What language do Mr. and Mrs. DiCarlo usually speak?
4. What language does Joe usually speak?
5. What do Mr. and Mrs. DiCarlo read?
6. What does Joe read?
7. What do Mr. and Mrs. DiCarlo listen to?
8. What does Joe listen to?
9. Where do Mr. and Mrs. DiCarlo shop?
10. Where does Joe shop?

WHICH WORD IS CORRECT?

1. Mrs. DiCarlo (read reads) the Italian newspaper.
2. Mr. DiCarlo (shop shops) at the Italian grocery store.
3. They (live lives) in New York City.
4. Joe (live lives) outside the city.
5. He (speak speaks) English.
6. Mr. and Mrs. DiCarlo (listen listens) to the radio.
7. They (visit visits) their friends every day.
8. Their friends (talk talks) about life back in "the old country."
9. Joe (call calls) his parents on the telephone.
10. Joe's friends (speak speaks) English.

LISTENING

Listen and choose the correct answer.

1. a. live b. lives
2. a. work b. works
3. a. speak b. speaks
4. a. drive b. drives
5. a. read b. reads
6. a. visit b. visits
7. a. cook b. cooks
8. a. paint b. paints
9. a. call b. calls
10. a. shop b. shops

How to Say It!

Hesitating

A. What do you do every day?

B. Hmm. Well . . .
I *work*, I *read the newspaper*, and I *visit my friends*.

Practice conversations with other students. Hesitate while you're thinking of your answer.

IN YOUR OWN WORDS

MRS. KOWALSKI

Mrs. Kowalski lives in an old Polish neighborhood in Chicago. She's upset about her son, Michael, and his wife, Kathy. Using the story on page 83 as a model, tell a story about Mrs. Kowalski.

INTERVIEW

Where do you live?
What language do you speak?
What do you do every day?

Interview another student.

?

I live in an apartment in the city.
I speak Spanish and a little English.
I go to school and visit my friends.

Then tell the class about that person.

She lives in an apartment in the city.
She speaks Spanish and a little English.
She goes to school and visits her friends.

PRONUNCIATION Blending with *does*

Listen. Then say it.	Say it. Then listen.
Where does he work?	Where does he shop?
Where does she live?	Where does she eat?
What does he do?	What does he cook?
What does she read?	What does she talk about?

Where do you live? What language do you speak? What do you do every day? Write a paragraph about it in your journal.

GRAMMAR FOCUS

Simple Present Tense

Where	do	I we you they	live?
	does	he she it	

I We You They	live	in Rome.
He She It	lives	

Match the questions and answers.

___ 1. Where do you and your wife live? a. They live in Mexico City.
___ 2. Where does your brother live? b. I live in Chicago.
___ 3. Where do your parents live? c. She lives in Los Angeles.
___ 4. Where does your sister live? d. We live in Dallas.
___ 5. Where do you live? e. He lives in London.

Choose the correct word.

6. He (drive drives) a truck.
7. We (speak speaks) Portuguese.
8. I (sell sells) cars.
9. They (read reads) every day.
10. Where (do does) they live?
11. Where (do does) she work?
12. You (speak speaks) Arabic.
13. She (listen listens) to the radio.
14. Where (do does) you work?
15. What language (do does) you and your wife speak?

10

Simple Present Tense: Yes/No Questions Negatives Short Answers

- Habitual Actions
- People's Interests and Activities

Vocabulary Preview

① SUN	② MON	③ TUE	④ WED	⑤ THU	⑥ FRI	⑦ SAT
1	2	3	4	5	6	7
8	9	10	11	12	13	14
15	16	17	18	19	20	21
22	23	24	25	26	27	28
29	30	31				

1. Sunday
2. Monday
3. Tuesday
4. Wednesday
5. Thursday
6. Friday
7. Saturday
8. baby-sit
9. clean
10. do yoga
11. go dancing
12. jog
13. play volleyball
14. ride
15. see a movie
16. see a play

Stanley's International Restaurant

He cooks.
He doesn't cook.
(does not)

Does he cook?
Yes, he does.
No, he doesn't.

What kind of food } does he cook?
When }

Stanley's International Restaurant is a very special place. Every day Stanley cooks a different kind of food. On Monday he cooks Italian food. On Tuesday he cooks Greek food. On Wednesday he cooks Chinese food. On Thursday he cooks Puerto Rican food. On Friday he cooks Japanese food. On Saturday he cooks Mexican food. And on Sunday he cooks American food.

A. What kind of food does Stanley cook on **Monday**?

B. On **Monday** he cooks **Italian** food.

Ask and answer questions about the other days of the week.

A. Does Stanley cook **Greek** food on **Tuesday**?

B. Yes, he does.

Ask six questions with "yes" answers.

A. Does Stanley cook **Japanese** food on **Sunday**?

B. No, he doesn't.

A. When does he cook **Japanese** food?

B. He cooks **Japanese** food on **Friday**.

Ask six questions with "no" answers.

You go.
You don't go.
(do not)

Do you go?
Yes, I do. / Yes, we do.
No, I don't. / No, we don't.

When do you go?

A. Do you go to Stanley's Restaurant on **Wednesday**?
B. Yes, I do.
A. Why?
B. Because I like **Chinese** food.

Ask these people.

1. *Monday?*

2. *Thursday?*

3. *Saturday?*

4. *Sunday?*

A. Do you go to Stanley's Restaurant on **Sunday**?
B. No, I don't.
A. Why not?
B. Because I don't like **American** food.

Ask these people.

5. *Tuesday?*

6. *Wednesday?*

7. *Friday?*

8. *Monday?*

A. What kind of food do you like?
B. I like **Russian** food.
A. When do you go to Stanley's Restaurant?
B. I don't go there.
A. Why not?
B. Because Stanley doesn't cook **Russian** food.

Ask these people.

9. *French*

10. *Ethiopian*

11. *Thai*

12. *Vietnamese*

Busy People!

Jeff is a very athletic person. He does a different kind of exercise or sport every day. On Monday he jogs. On Tuesday he plays tennis. On Wednesday he does yoga. On Thursday he swims. On Friday he goes to a health club. On Saturday he plays basketball. And on Sunday he rides his bike.

Julie is a very busy student. She does a different activity every day. On Monday she sings in the choir. On Tuesday she plays in the orchestra. On Wednesday she writes for the school newspaper. On Thursday she plays volleyball. On Friday she baby-sits for her neighbors. On Saturday she works at the mall. And on Sunday she visits her grandparents.

Mr. and Mrs. Baker are very active people. They do something different every day of the week. On Monday they go to a museum. On Tuesday they see a play. On Wednesday they go to a concert. On Thursday they take a karate lesson. On Friday they go dancing. On Saturday they see a movie. And on Sunday they play cards with their friends.

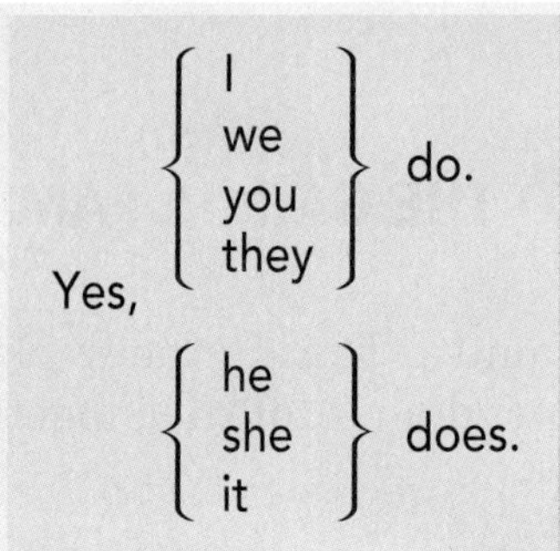

Yes, { I / we / you / they } do.

Yes, { he / she / it } does.

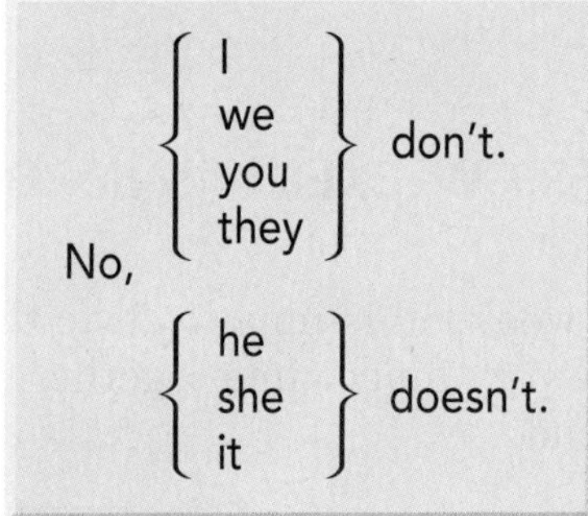

No, { I / we / you / they } don't.

No, { he / she / it } doesn't.

A. Does Jeff play tennis on Tuesday?

B. Yes, he does.

A. Does Julie work at the mall on Saturday?

B. Yes, she does.

A. Do Mr. and Mrs. Baker go dancing on Friday?

B. Yes, they do.

Ask other questions with "yes" answers.

A. Does Jeff do yoga on Sunday?

B. No, he doesn't.

A. Does Julie sing in the choir on Thursday?

B. No, she doesn't.

A. Do Mr. and Mrs. Baker see a movie on Monday?

B. No, they don't.

Ask other questions with "no" answers.

Do you swim on Thursday?
Yes, I do.
Do you play volleyball on Sunday?
No, I don't.
Do you go dancing on Friday?
Yes, we do.
Do you see a play on Monday?
No, we don't.

Now interview Jeff, Julie, and Mr. and Mrs. Baker. Practice conversations with other students.

READING

EVERY WEEKEND IS IMPORTANT TO THE GARCIA FAMILY

Every weekend is important to the Garcia family. During the week they don't have very much time together, but they spend a LOT of time together on the weekend.

Mr. Garcia works at the post office during the week, but he doesn't work there on the weekend. Mrs. Garcia works at the bank during the week, but she doesn't work there on the weekend. Jennifer and Jonathan Garcia go to school during the week, but they don't go to school on the weekend. And the Garcias' dog, Max, stays home alone during the week, but he doesn't stay home alone on the weekend.

On Saturday and Sunday the Garcias spend time together. On Saturday morning they clean the house together. On Saturday afternoon they work in the garden together. And on Saturday evening they watch videos together. On Sunday morning they go to church together. On Sunday afternoon they have a big dinner together. And on Sunday evening they play their musical instruments together.

As you can see, every weekend is special to the Garcias. It's their only time together as a family.

✓ READING *CHECK-UP*

Q & A

Using these models, make questions and answers based on the story on page 92.

A. What *does Mr. Garcia* do during the week?
B. *He works at the post office.*

A. What do the Garcias do on *Saturday morning*?
B. They *clean the house* together.

WHAT'S THE ANSWER?

1. Does Mr. Garcia work at the post office?
2. Do Jennifer and Jonathan go to school during the week?
3. Does Mrs. Garcia work at the post office?
4. Do Mr. and Mrs. Garcia have much time together during the week?
5. Does Jennifer watch videos on Saturday evening?
6. Do Jennifer and her brother clean the house on Saturday morning?
7. Does Mr. Garcia work in the garden on Saturday evening?

DO OR DOES?

1. _____Mr. Garcia work on the weekend?
2. _____ Jennifer and Jonathan go to school during the week?
3. When _____ they watch videos?
4. Where _____ Mrs. Garcia work?
5. _____ you speak Spanish?
6. What _____ Mr. Garcia do during the week?

DON'T OR DOESN'T?

1. Mr. and Mrs. Garcia _____ work on the weekend.
2. Jennifer _____ work at the bank.
3. We _____ watch videos during the week.
4. My son _____ play a musical instrument.
5. My sister and I _____ eat at Stanley's Restaurant.
6. Our dog _____ like our neighbor's dog.

LISTENING

WHAT'S THE WORD?

Listen and choose the word you hear.

1. a. do b. does
2. a. do b. does
3. a. Sunday b. Monday
4. a. don't b. doesn't
5. a. don't b. doesn't
6. a. does b. goes
7. a. Tuesday b. Thursday
8. a. go b. don't

WHAT'S THE ANSWER?

Listen and choose the correct response.

1. a. Yes, I do. b. Yes, he does.
2. a. Yes, they do. b. Yes, she does.
3. a. No, she doesn't. b. No, we don't.
4. a. No, he doesn't. b. No, we don't.
5. a. No, I don't. b. No, he doesn't.
6. a. No, I don't. b. No, they don't.
7. a. Yes, we do. b. Yes, they do.
8. a. Yes, they do. b. Yes, he does.

How About You?

Tell about yourself:
What do you do during the week?
What do you do on the weekend?

Now tell about another person—a friend, someone in your family, or another student:
What does he/she do during the week?
What does he/she do on the weekend?

READING

A VERY OUTGOING PERSON

Alice is a very outgoing person. She spends a lot of time with her friends. She goes to parties, she goes to movies, and she goes to concerts. She's very popular.

She also likes sports very much. She plays basketball, she plays baseball, and she plays volleyball. She's very athletic.

Alice doesn't stay home alone very often. She doesn't read many books, she doesn't watch TV, and she doesn't listen to music. She's very active.

As you can see, Alice is a very outgoing person.

IN YOUR OWN WORDS

FOR WRITING AND DISCUSSION

A VERY SHY PERSON

Using the story about Alice as a model, tell a story about Sheldon. Begin your story:

Sheldon is a very shy person. He doesn't spend a lot of time with his friends. He doesn't go . . .

Tell about yourself:

What kind of person are you?

Are you outgoing? shy? active? athletic?

Tell how you spend your time.

How to Say It!

Starting a Conversation

A. Tell me, what kind of *movies* do you like?
B. I like *comedies*.
A. Who's your favorite *movie star*?
B. *Tim Kelly*.

Practice the interviews on this page, using "Tell me" to start the conversations.

INTERVIEW

First, answer these questions about yourself. Next, interview another student. Then, tell the class about yourself and the other student.

1. What kind of movies do you like?
   Who's your favorite movie star?

comedies

dramas

westerns

adventure movies

science fiction movies

cartoons

2. What kind of books do you like?
   Who's your favorite author?

novels

poetry

short stories

non-fiction

biographies

3. What kind of TV programs do you like?
   Who's your favorite TV star?

comedies

dramas

cartoons

game shows

news programs

4. What kind of music do you like?
   Who's your favorite performer?

classical music

popular music

jazz

rock music

country music

5. What kind of sports do you like?
   Who's your favorite athlete? What's your favorite team?

football

baseball

soccer

golf

hockey

tennis

PRONUNCIATION Reduced *of*

Listen. Then say it.

What kind of movies do you like?

What kind of books do you like?

She spends a lot of time with her friends.

Say it. Then listen.

What kind of music do you like?

What kind of TV programs do you like?

I read a lot of books.

What do you do during the week?
What do you do on the weekend?
Write about it in your journal.

GRAMMAR FOCUS

Simple Present Tense: Yes/No Questions

Do	I we you they	work?
Does	he she it	

Short Answers

Yes,	I we you they	do.
	he she it	does.

No,	I we you they	don't.
	he she it	doesn't.

Complete the sentences.

1. A. _______ you and your wife like Italian food?
   B. Yes, we _______.
2. A. _______ your brother work at the mall?
   B. Yes, he _______.
3. A. _______ your friends play cards?
   B. No, they _______.
4. A. _______ you play a musical instrument?
   B. Yes, I _______.
5. A. _______ your sister take karate lessons?
   B. No, she _______.
6. A. _______ I ask a lot of questions?
   B. Yes, you _______.
7. A. _______ you and your husband play golf?
   B. No, _______ _______.
8. A. _______ your uncle speak French?
   B. No, _______ _______.
9. A. Do your neighbors make a lot of noise?
   B. Yes, _______ _______.
10. A. _______ your daughter speak Chinese?
    B. Yes, _______ _______.

Simple Present Tense: Negatives

I We You They	don't	work.
He She It	doesn't	

Complete the sentences with *don't* or *doesn't*.

11. I _______ work on Sunday.
12. My husband _______ play tennis.
13. My parents _______ go dancing.
14. My sister and I _______ sing in the choir.
15. My wife _______ watch TV.
16. You _______ like hockey.

SIDE by SIDE Gazette

Volume 1 Number 4

Language

Millions speak Chinese. Only hundreds speak Bahinemo.

There are over 20,000 languages in the world. Some of these languages are very common. For example, millions of people speak Chinese, Spanish, English, Arabic, Portuguese, and Japanese. On the other hand, some languages are very rare. For example, only 500 people in Papua, New Guinea speak the language Bahinemo.

Languages grow and change. They borrow words from other languages. For example, in the English language, the word *rodeo* is from Spanish, *cafe* comes from French, *ketchup* is from Chinese, *sofa* is from Arabic, and *potato* comes from Haitian Kreyol. New words also come from technology. For example, *cyberspace*, *website*, and *e-mail* are recent words that relate to the Internet.

FACT FILE

Common Languages

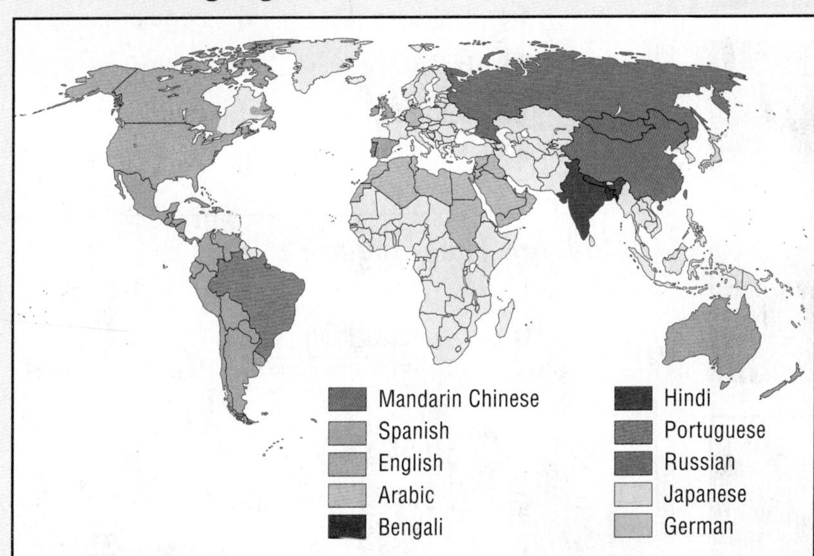

Language	Number of Speakers	Language	Number of Speakers
Mandarin Chinese	885 million	Hindi	182 million
Spanish	332 million	Portuguese	170 million
English	322 million	Russian	170 million
Arabic	268 million	Japanese	125 million
Bengali	189 million	German	98 million

BUILD YOUR VOCABULARY!

Everyday Activities

Every day I ________ .

■ get up

■ take a shower

■ brush my teeth

■ comb my hair

■ get dressed

■ go to school

■ go to work

■ eat

■ take a bath

■ go to bed

AROUND THE WORLD

Exercising

People around the world exercise in different ways.

Some people exercise in health clubs.

Some people exercise at the beach.

Some people go hiking.

And some people exercise together outdoors.

How do people exercise in your country?

Global Exchange

Jogger9: I'm a very active person. I jog and I swim. I go to a lot of movies and concerts. I sing in a choir. I play basketball with my friends every weekend. I like rock music and jazz. I don't watch TV very often. I only watch news programs. I read a lot of books. I like novels. My favorite author is Tom Clancy. How about you? Tell me about your activities and interests.

Send a message to a keypal. Tell about your activities and interests.

LISTENING

Hello! This Is the International Cafe!

c	1	Monday	a.	jazz
___	2	Tuesday	b.	rock music
___	3	Wednesday	c.	classical music
___	4	Thursday	d.	popular music
___	5	Friday	e.	poetry
___	6	Saturday	f.	country music
___	7	Sunday	g.	short stories

What Are They Saying?

11

Object Pronouns
Simple Present Tense: -*s* vs. non-*s* Endings
Have/Has
Adverbs of Frequency

- Describing Frequency of Actions
- Describing People

Vocabulary Preview

1. year
2. month
3. week
4. day
5. weekend
6. morning
7. afternoon
8. evening
9. night

How Often?

I	me
he	him
she	her
it	it
we	us
you	you
they	them

A. How often does your boyfriend call you?

B. He calls me every night.

1. How often do you use your computer?
   every day

2. How often do you write to your son?
   every week

3. How often do you clean your windows?
   every month

4. How often do you visit your aunt in Minnesota?
   every year

5. How often do you wash your car?
   every weekend

6. How often do your grandchildren call you?
   every Sunday

7. How often does your boss say "hello" to you?
   every morning

8. How often do you feed the animals?
   every afternoon

9. How often do you think about me?
   all the time

She Usually Studies in the Library

[s]		[z]		[ɪz]			
eat	eats	read	reads	wash	washes	always	100%
write	writes	jog	jogs	watch	watches	usually	90%
bark	barks	call	calls	dance	dances	sometimes	50%
speak	speaks	clean	cleans	fix	fixes	rarely	10%
						never	0%

A. Does Carmen usually study in her room?

B. No. She rarely studies in her room. She usually studies in the library.

1. Does Linda usually eat lunch in her office?
rarely
in the cafeteria

2. Does Alan always watch the news after dinner?
never
game shows

3. Does Diane sometimes read *The National Star*?
never
Time magazine

4. Does Henry usually wash his car on Sunday?
rarely
on Saturday

5. Does your girlfriend usually jog in the evening?
sometimes
in the afternoon

6. Does your neighbor's dog always bark during the day?
never
at night

We Have Noisy Neighbors

I We You They	have	brown eyes.
He She It	has	

A. Do you have quiet neighbors?

B. No. We have noisy neighbors.

1. Do you have a sister?
a brother

2. Does this store have an elevator?
an escalator

3. Does your daughter have straight hair?
curly hair

4. Does your son have brown hair?
blond hair

5. Do you and your husband have a dog?
a cat

6. Does your baby boy have blue eyes?
brown eyes

7. Do Mr. and Mrs. Hill have a satellite dish?
an old TV antenna

8. Does your grandmother have a car?
a motorcycle

9.

ON YOUR OWN *Very Different*

My brother and I look very different. I have brown eyes and he has blue eyes. We both have brown hair, but I have short, curly hair and he has long, straight hair. I'm tall and thin. He's short and heavy.

As you can see, I don't look like my brother. We look very different.

Who in your family do you look like? Who DON'T you look like? Tell about it.

My sister and I are very different. I'm a teacher. She's a journalist. I live in Miami. She lives in London. I have a large house in the suburbs. She has a small apartment in the city.

I'm married. She's single. I play golf. She plays tennis. I play the piano. She doesn't play a musical instrument. On the weekend I usually watch videos and rarely go out. She never watches videos and always goes to parties.

As you can see, we're very different. But we're sisters . . . and we're friends.

Compare yourself with a member of your family, another student in your class, or a famous person. Tell how you and this person are different.

How to Say It!

Reacting to Information

A. Tell me about *your sister.*
B. *She's a journalist. She lives in London.*
A. Oh, really? That's interesting.

Practice conversations with other students. Talk about people you know.

READING

CLOSE FRIENDS

My husband and I are very lucky. We have many close friends in this city, and they're all interesting people.

Our friend Greta is an actress. We see her when she isn't making a movie in Hollywood. When we get together with her, she always tells us about her life in Hollywood as a movie star. Greta is a very close friend. We like her very much.

Our friend Dan is a scientist. We see him when he isn't busy in his laboratory. When we get together with him, he always tells us about his new experiments. Dan is a very close friend. We like him very much.

Our friends Bob and Carol are famous television news reporters. We see them when they aren't traveling around the world. When we get together with them, they always tell us about their conversations with presidents and prime ministers. Bob and Carol are very close friends. We like them very much.

Unfortunately, we don't see Greta, Dan, Bob, or Carol very often. In fact, we rarely see them because they're usually so busy. But we think about them all the time.

✓ READING *CHECK-UP*

WHAT'S THE WORD?

Greta is a famous actress. ________1 lives in Hollywood. ________2 movies are very popular. When ________3 walks down the street, people always say "hello" to ________4 and tell ________5 how much they like ________6 movies.

Dan is always busy. ________7 works in ________8 laboratory every day. Dan's friends rarely see ________9. When they see ________10, ________11 usually talks about ________12 experiments. Everybody likes ________13 very much. ________14 is a very nice person.

Bob and Carol are television news reporters. ________15 friends don't see ________16 very often because ________17 travel around the world all the time. Presidents and prime ministers often call ________18 on the telephone. ________19 like ________20 work very much.

LISTENING

Listen to the conversations. Who and what are they talking about?

1. a. grandfather
   b. grandmother
2. a. window
   b. windows
3. a. brother
   b. sister
4. a. sink
   b. cars
5. a. neighbor
   b. neighbors
6. a. computer
   b. news reporter
7. a. game show
   b. car
8. a. Ms. Brown
   b. Mr. Wong
9. a. Ken
   b. Jim and Karen

IN YOUR OWN WORDS

FOR WRITING AND DISCUSSION

MY CLOSE FRIENDS

Tell about your close friends.

What are their names?
Where do they live?
What do they do?
When do you get together with them?
What do you talk about?

PRONUNCIATION Deleted *h*

Listen. Then say it.

I visit her every year.

I write to him every week.

We see her very often.

She calls him every month.

Say it. Then listen.

I visit him every year.

I write to her every week.

We see him very often.

He calls her every month.

Write in your journal about your daily activities.

I always ______. I usually ______.

I sometimes ______. I rarely ______. I never ______.

GRAMMAR FOCUS

OBJECT PRONOUNS

He calls	me him her it us you them	every night.

Complete the sentences.

1. A. How often do you and your wife read the newspaper?
   B. We read ______ every morning.
2. A. How often do you write to your grandmother?
   B. I write to ______ every week.
3. A. How often do you call your brother in Miami?
   B. I call ______ every Sunday.
4. A. How often do the Baxters play cards with their friends?
   B. They play cards with ______ every Saturday night.
5. A. How often does your uncle call you and your sister?
   B. He calls ______ every weekend.

HAVE/HAS

I We You They	have	brown eyes.
He She It	has	

Complete the sentences with *have* or *has*.

6. We ______ noisy neighbors.
7. My son ______ brown eyes.
8. I ______ curly black hair.
9. My sister ______ a new car.
10. You ______ a very nice apartment.
11. My parents ______ a new cat.
12. The new mall ______ more than fifty stores.

SIMPLE PRESENT TENSE: *S* VS. NON-*S* ENDINGS

He She It	eats. reads. washes.	[s] [z] [ɪz]

I We You They	eat. read. wash.

Complete the sentences with the correct form of the verb.

13. (like) I ______ jazz. My brother ______ rock music.
14. (jog) My wife ______ in the morning. I ______ in the afternoon.
15. (study) I ______ in my room. My sister ______ in the library.
16. (watch) Our son ______ game shows after dinner. My wife and I ______ the news.

12

Contrast: Simple Present and Present Continuous Tenses

Adjectives

- Feelings and Emotions
- Describing Usual and Unusual Activities

Vocabulary Preview

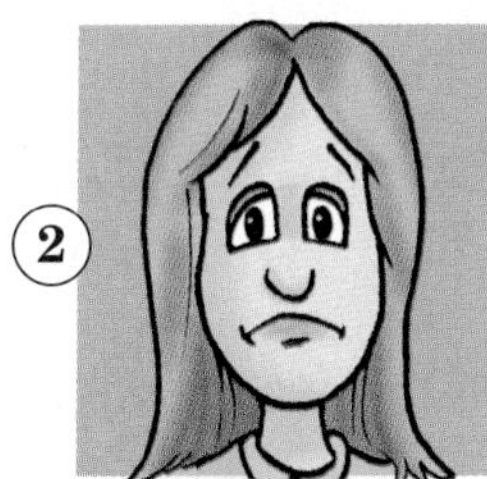

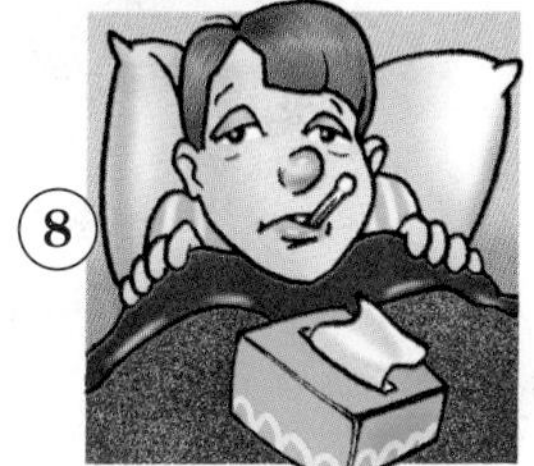

1. happy
2. sad
3. hungry
4. thirsty
5. hot
6. cold
7. tired
8. sick
9. angry
10. nervous
11. scared
12. embarrassed

I Always Cry When I'm Sad

cry
crying

A. Why are you crying?

B. I'm crying because I'm sad.
I ALWAYS cry when I'm sad.

smile
smiling

A. Why is she smiling?

B. She's smiling because she's happy.
She ALWAYS smiles when she's happy.

shout
shouting

1. A. Why are you shouting?

B. ____________ angry.

I ALWAYS ____________.

bite
biting

2. A. Why is he biting his nails?

B. ____________ nervous.

He ALWAYS ____________.

drink
drinking

3. A. Why is the bird drinking?

B. ____________ thirsty.

It ALWAYS ____________.

shiver
shivering

4. A. Why are they shivering?

B. ____________ cold.

They ALWAYS ____________.

go
going

5. A. Why are they going to Stanley's Restaurant?

B. ____________ hungry.

They ALWAYS ____________.

go
going

6. A. Why is she going to the doctor?

B. ____________ sick.

She ALWAYS ____________.

perspire
perspiring

7. **A.** Why are you perspiring?
   B. ____________ hot.
   I ALWAYS ____________.

blush
blushing

8. **A.** Why is he blushing?
   B. ____________ embarrassed.
   He ALWAYS ____________.

yawn
yawning

9. **A.** Why is she yawning?
   B. ____________ tired.
   She ALWAYS ____________.

cover
covering

10. **A.** Why is he covering his eyes?
    B. ____________ scared.
    He ALWAYS ____________.

ON YOUR OWN *What Do You Do When You're Nervous?*

What do you do when you're nervous?

When I'm nervous, I perspire.

When I'm nervous, I bite my nails.

When I'm nervous, I walk back and forth.

Answer these questions.

What do you do when you're . . .

1. nervous?
2. sad?
3. happy?
4. tired?
5. sick?
6. cold?
7. hot?
8. hungry?
9.  thirsty?
10. angry?
11.  embarrassed?
12. scared?

Now ask another student in your class.

I'm Washing the Dishes in the Bathtub

A. What are you doing?!

B. I'm washing the dishes in the bathtub.

A. That's strange! Do you USUALLY wash the dishes in the bathtub?

B. No. I NEVER wash the dishes in the bathtub, but I'm washing the dishes in the bathtub TODAY.

A. Why are you doing THAT?!

B. Because my sink is broken.

A. I'm sorry to hear that.

A. What are you doing?!
B. I'm ________.
A. That's strange! Do you USUALLY ________?
B. No. I NEVER ________, but I'm ________ TODAY.
A. Why are you doing THAT?!
B. Because my ________ is broken.
A. I'm sorry to hear that.

1. *sleep* / *sleeping* } *on the floor*
   bed

2. *study* / *studying* } *with a flashlight*
   lamp

3. *walk* / *walking* } *to work*
   car

4. *use* / *using* } *a typewriter*
   computer

5. *sweep* / *sweeping* } *the carpet*
   vacuum

6.

How to Say It!

Reacting to Bad News

A. *My sink is broken.*

B. { I'm sorry to hear that.
That's too bad!
What a shame! }

Practice conversations with other students. Share some bad news and react to it.

READING

A BAD DAY AT THE OFFICE

Mr. Blaine is the president of the Acme Internet Company. The company has a staff of energetic employees. Unfortunately, all of the employees are out today. Nobody is there. As a result, Mr. Blaine is doing everybody's job, and he's having a VERY bad day at the office!

He's answering the telephone because the receptionist who usually answers it is at the dentist's office. He's typing letters because the secretary who usually types them is at home in bed with the flu. He's sorting the mail because the office assistant who usually sorts it is on vacation. And he's even cleaning the office because the custodian who usually cleans it is on strike.

Poor Mr. Blaine! It's a very busy day at the Acme Internet Company, and nobody is there to help him. He's having a VERY bad day at the office!

READING *CHECK-UP*

TRUE OR FALSE?

1. Mr. Blaine is the president of the Ajax Internet Company.
2. Mr. Blaine is out today.
3. The secretary is sick.
4. The office assistant is on strike.
5. The custodian isn't cleaning the office today.
6. The receptionist usually answers the phone at the dentist's office.

LISTENING

Listen and choose the correct answer.

1. a. I clean my house.
   b. I'm cleaning my house.
2. a. He sorts the mail.
   b. He's sorting the mail.
3. a. She answers the telephone.
   b. She's answering the telephone.
4. a. Yes. He yawns.
   b. Yes. He's yawning.
5. a. I'm covering my eyes.
   b. I cover my eyes.
6. a. I study in the library.
   b. I'm studying in the library.

READING

EARLY MONDAY MORNING IN CENTERVILLE

Early Monday morning is usually a very busy time in Centerville. Men and women usually rush to their jobs. Some people walk to work, some people drive, and others take the bus. Children usually go to school. Some children walk to school, some children take the school bus, and others ride their bicycles. The city is usually very busy. Trucks deliver food to supermarkets, mail carriers deliver mail to homes and businesses, and police officers direct traffic at every corner. Yes, early Monday morning is usually a very busy time in Centerville.

✓ READING *CHECK-UP*

Using the story above as a guide, complete the following:

THE SNOWSTORM

Today isn't a typical early Monday morning in Centerville. In fact, it's a very unusual morning. It's snowing very hard there. All the people are at home. The streets are empty, and the city is quiet. The men and women who usually rush to their jobs aren't rushing to their jobs today. The people who usually walk to work aren't walking, the people who usually drive aren't ________1, and the people who usually take the bus aren't ________2 the bus. The children who usually go to school aren't ________3 to school today. The children who usually walk to school aren't ________4 today. The children who usually ________5 the school bus aren't ________6 it today. And the children who usually ________7 their bicycles aren't ________8 them this morning.

The city is very quiet. The trucks that usually ________9 food aren't ________10 it today. The mail carriers who usually ________11 mail aren't ________12 it this morning. And the police officers who usually ________13 traffic aren't ________14 it today. Yes, it's a very unusual Monday morning in Centerville.

PRONUNCIATION Reduced *to*

Listen. Then say it.

I'm sorry to hear that.

We go to school.

He listens to the radio.

Mail carriers deliver mail to homes.

Say it. Then listen.

I'm happy to hear that.

They're going to the doctor.

She listens to music.

Trucks deliver food to supermarkets.

Describe a typical day in your city or town. What do people usually do? Write about it in your journal.

GRAMMAR FOCUS

Simple Present Tense

I always **cry** when I'm sad.

I never **wash** the dishes in the bathtub.

Present Continuous Tense

I'm crying because I'm sad.

I'm washing the dishes in the bathtub today.

Complete the sentences with the correct form of the verb.

bite biting	clean cleaning	shiver shivering	smile smiling	walk walking
blush blushing	cry crying	shout shouting	use using	yawn yawning

1. I often ________ when I'm sad.
2. Why are you ________? Are you angry?
3. Carol is ________. She's very tired.
4. He's ________ because he's happy.
5. I'm ________ my office today because the people who usually ________ it are on strike.
6. When I'm nervous, I ________ my nails.
7. I ________ when I'm embarrassed.
8. Why are you ________ a typewriter today?
9. I usually ________ when I'm very cold.
10. I don't usually ________ to work, but I'm ________ to work today.

SIDE by SIDE Gazette

Volume 1 Number 5

Traffic: A Global Problem

There are more and more people and more and more cars

Traffic is a big problem in many cities around the world. Traffic is especially bad during *rush hour*—the time when people go to work or school and the time when they go home. Many people take buses, subways, or trains to work, but many other people drive their cars. As a result, the streets are very busy, and traffic is very bad.

Many cities are trying to solve their traffic problems. Some cities are building more roads. Other cities are expanding their bus and subway systems.

Many cities are trying to reduce the number of cars on their roads. Some highways have *carpool lanes*—special lanes for cars with two, three, or more people. In some cities, people drive their cars only on certain days of the week. For example, in Athens, people with license plate numbers ending in 0 through 4 drive on some days, and people with numbers ending in 5 through 9 drive on other days.

Every day around the world, more and more people drive to and from work in more and more cars. As a result, traffic is a global problem.

LISTENING

TODAY'S NEWS

And Now, Here's Today's News!

b	1 There's a subway problem in . . .	a.	Toronto
___	2 Police officers are on strike in . . .	b.	Boston
___	3 It's snowing very hard in . . .	c.	Miami
___	4 There aren't any problems in . . .	d.	Sacramento
___	5 Children aren't going to school in . . .	e.	Chicago

BUILD YOUR VOCABULARY!

How Do You Get to Work?

I ________ .

■ walk

■ drive

■ take the bus

■ take the train

■ take the subway

■ take a taxi

■ ride a bicycle

■ ride a motor scooter

■ ride a motorcycle

AROUND THE WORLD

Getting Places

People around the world go to work or school in many different ways.

Some people take the subway.

Some people ride a bicycle.

Some people ride a motor scooter.

Some people even roller-blade!

How do people go to work or school in different countries you know?

FACT FILE

World's Largest Subway Systems

City	Number of Riders in a Year (in millions)	City	Number of Riders in a Year (in millions)
Moscow	3,160	Paris	1,120
Tokyo	2,740	Osaka	1,000
Mexico City	1,420	Hong Kong	779
Seoul	1,390	London	770
New York	1,130	Sao Paulo	701

Global Exchange

JeffZ: I live in a small apartment in the center of our city. I have a brother and two sisters. My brother's name is Kevin, and my sisters' names are Emily and Melissa. Our family has a dog and a bird. Our dog's name is Buster, and our bird's name is Lulu. I'm tall, and I have brown eyes. My hair is short and curly. It's usually black, but this week it's red. How about you? Where do you live? Do you have brothers or sisters? What are their names? Do you have a dog or a cat or another pet? What do you look like?

Send a message to a keypal. Tell about yourself.

What Are They Saying?

13

Can
Have to

- Expressing Ability
- Occupations
- Looking for a Job
- Expressing Obligation
- Invitations

Vocabulary Preview

1. actor
2. actress
3. baker
4. chef
5. construction worker
6. dancer
7. mechanic
8. salesperson
9. secretary
10. singer
11. superintendent
12. teacher
13. truck driver

Can You?

I He She It We You They	can/can't sing. (cannot)

Can you sing?
Yes, I can.
No, I can't.

Can you speak Hungarian?
No, I can't. But I can speak Romanian.

1. Can Betty drive a bus?

2. Can Fred cook Italian food?

3. Can they ski?

4. Can you skate?

5. Can Roger use a cash register?

6. Can Judy and Donna play baseball?

7. Can Rita play the trumpet?

8. Can Marvin paint pictures?

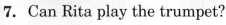

Ask another student in your class: "Can you _____?"

Of Course They Can

A. Can Jack fix cars?

B. Of course he can.
He fixes cars every day. He's a mechanic.

1. Can Michael type?
secretary

2. Can Barbara teach?
teacher

3. Can Oscar bake pies and cakes?
baker

4. Can Jane drive a truck?
truck driver

5. Can Stanley cook?
chef

6. Can Claudia sing?
singer

7. Can Bruce and Helen dance?
dancers

8. Can Arthur act?
actor

9. Can Elizabeth and Katherine act?
actresses

READING

THE ACE EMPLOYMENT SERVICE

Many people are sitting in the reception room at the Ace Employment Service. They're all looking for work, and they're hoping they can find jobs today.

Natalie is looking for a job as a secretary. She can type, she can file, and she can use business software on the computer. William is looking for a job as a building superintendent. He can paint walls, he can repair locks, and he can fix stoves and refrigerators.

Sandra is looking for a job as a construction worker. She can use tools, she can operate equipment, and she can build things. Nick is looking for a job as a salesperson. He can talk to customers, he can use a cash register, and he can take inventory. Stephanie and Tiffany are looking for jobs as actresses. They can sing, they can dance, and they can act.

Good luck, everybody! We hope you find the jobs you're looking for!

✓ READING *CHECK-UP*

Q & A

Natalie, William, Sandra, Nick, Stephanie, and Tiffany are having their interviews at the Ace Employment Service. Using this model, create dialogs based on the story.

A. What's your name?
B. *Natalie Kramer.*
A. Nice to meet you. Tell me, *Natalie*, what kind of job are you looking for?
B. I'm looking for a job as *a secretary*.
A. Tell me about your skills. What can you do?
B. I can *type*, I can *file*, and I can *use business software on the computer*.

LISTENING

CAN OR CAN'T?

Listen and choose the word you hear.

1. a. can b. can't
2. a. can b. can't
3. a. can b. can't
4. a. can b. can't
5. a. can b. can't
6. a. can b. can't

WHAT CAN THEY DO?

Listen and choose what each person can do.

1. a. file b. type
2. a. cook b. bake
3. a. repair locks b. repair stoves
4. a. drive a truck b. drive a bus
5. a. teach French b. teach English
6. a. take inventory b. paint

ON YOUR OWN *Your Skills*

Think about your skills. What can you do? What CAN'T you do? Make two lists. Then talk about your lists with other students.

Things I Can Do	Things I Can't Do
....	....
....	....
....	....
....	....
....	....

They Can't Go to Herbert's Party

I
We
You
They
have to
work.
He
She
It
has to

Herbert is depressed. He's having a party today, but his friends can't go to his party. They're all busy.

A. Can you go to Herbert's party?

B. No, I can't. I have to work.

A. Can Michael go to Herbert's party?

B. No, he can't. He has to go to the doctor.

1. *you and Tom?*
fix our car

2. *Susan?*
go to the dentist

3. *your children?*
do their homework

4. *John?*
wash his clothes

5. *your parents?*
clean their apartment

6. Can YOU go to Herbert's party?

How to Say It!

Apologizing

A. Can you *go to a movie* with me on *Saturday*?
B. I'm sorry. I can't. I have to *clean my apartment*.

Practice the interactions on this page, using "I'm sorry" to apologize.

INTERACTIONS

A. Can you ____________ with me on ____________?
B. I'm sorry. I can't. I have to ____________.

Practice conversations with other students. Practice inviting, apologizing, and giving reasons.

go to a soccer game

have lunch

have dinner

go swimming

go shopping

go dancing

go skating

go skiing

go bowling

APPLYING FOR A DRIVER'S LICENSE

Henry is annoyed. He's applying for a driver's license, and he's upset about all the things he has to do.

First, he has to go to the Motor Vehicles Department and pick up an application form. He can't ask for the form on the telephone, and he can't ask for it by mail. He has to go downtown and pick up the form in person.

He has to fill out the form in duplicate. He can't use a pencil. He has to use a pen. He can't use blue ink. He has to use black ink. And he can't write in script. He has to print.

He also has to attach two photographs to the application. They can't be old photographs. They have to be new. They can't be large. They have to be small. And they can't be black and white. They have to be color.

Then he has to submit his application. He has to wait in a long line to pay his application fee. He has to wait in another long line to have an eye examination. And believe it or not, he has to wait in ANOTHER long line to take a written test!

Finally, he has to take a road test. He has to start the car. He has to make a right turn, a left turn, and a U-turn. And he even has to park his car on a crowded city street.

No wonder Henry is annoyed! He's applying for his driver's license, and he can't believe all the things he has to do.

✓ READING *CHECK-UP*

WHAT'S THE ANSWER?

1. Can Henry apply for a driver's license on the telephone?
2. Where does he have to go to apply for a license?
3. How does he have to fill out the form?
4. How many photographs does he have to attach to the application?
5. What kind of photographs do they have to be?
6. What does Henry have to do during the road test?

FIX THIS SIGN!

This sign at the Motor Vehicles Department is wrong. The things people have to do are in the wrong order. On a separate sheet of paper, fix the sign based on the story.

How to Apply for a Driver's License

Have an eye examination.
Pay the application fee.
Take a road test.
Pick up an application form.
Take a written test.
Fill out the form in duplicate.

IN YOUR OWN WORDS

FOR WRITING AND DISCUSSION

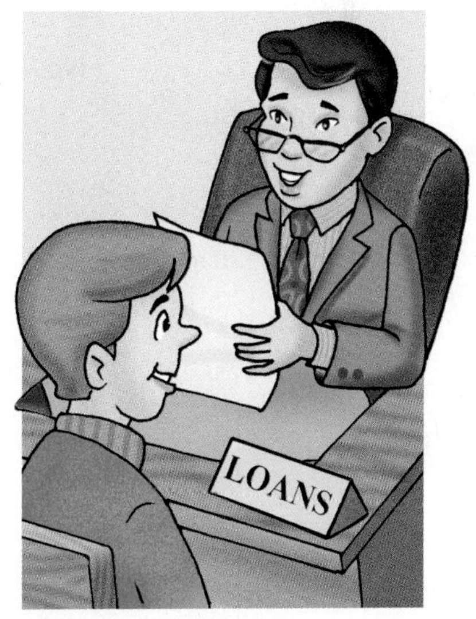

Explain how to apply for one of the following: a passport, a marriage license, a loan, or something else. In your explanation, use "You have to."*

* "You have to" = "A person has to"

PRONUNCIATION *Can & Can't*

Listen. Then say it.

I can type.

She can teach.

Yes, I can.

No, he can't.

Say it. Then listen.

We can dance.

He can sing.

Yes, they can.

No, she can't.

What do you have to do this week? Write about it in your journal.

GRAMMAR FOCUS

Can

Can	I he she it we you they	sing?

I He She It We You They	can can't	sing.

Yes,	I he she it we you they	can.

No,	I he she it we you they	can't.

Complete the sentences with *can* or *can't*.

1. I _____ bake. I'm a very good baker.
2. Gregory is a very bad singer. He _____ sing.
3. Maria can't ski, but she _____ skate.
4. We _____ dance. We aren't good dancers.
5. They can play baseball, but they _____ play tennis.
6. A. _____ you drive a truck?
   B. Yes, I _____.
7. A. _____ your brother fix cars?
   B. No, he _____.
8. A. _____ she repair stoves?
   B. No, she _____, but she _____ repair locks.

Have to

I We You They	have to	work.
He She It	has to	

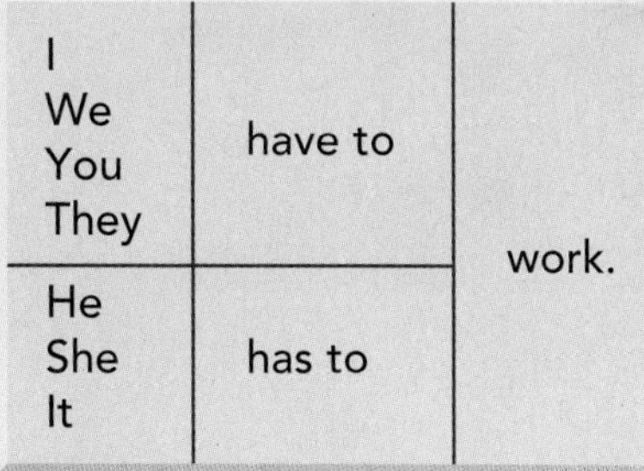

Complete the sentences with *have to* or *has to*.

9. I can't go to your party. I _______ work.
10. Beth _______ go to the dentist today.
11. Mr. and Mrs. Shen _______ clean their apartment today.
12. Ruben _______ wash his clothes today.
13. We can't go swimming. We _______ fix our car.
14. Bobby, you can't go skating. You _______ do your homework.

Future: Going to
Time Expressions
Want to

- Describing Future Plans and Intentions
- Expressing Wants
- Weather Forecasts
- Telling Time
- Making Predictions

Vocabulary Preview

Time

2:00
It's two o'clock.

2:15
It's two fifteen.
It's a quarter after two.

2:30
It's two thirty.
It's half past two.

2:45
It's two forty-five.
It's a quarter to three.

Months of the Year

Seasons

spring

summer

fall/autumn

winter

What Are They Going to Do Tomorrow?

What	am	I	going to do?
	is	he she it	
	are	we you they	

(I am)	I'm	going to read.
(He is)	He's	
(She is)	She's	
(It is)	It's	
(We are)	We're	
(You are)	You're	
(They are)	They're	

A. What's Fred going to do tomorrow?

B. He's going to fix his car.

1. *Jenny?*

2. *Cathy and Dave?*

3. *Tony?*

4. *you and your brother?*

5. *Andrew?*

6. *Ashley?*

They're Going to the Beach

They're going (to go) to the beach.	=	They're going to the beach. They're going to go to the beach.
We're going (to go) swimming.	=	We're going swimming. We're going to go swimming.

today	*tomorrow*
this morning	tomorrow morning
this afternoon	tomorrow afternoon
this evening	tomorrow evening
tonight	tomorrow night

A. What are Mr. and Mrs. Brown going to do tomorrow?

B. They're going (to go) to the beach.

1. What's Anita going to do this morning?

2. What are Steve and Brenda going to do tonight?

3. What's Fernando going to do tomorrow evening?

4. What are you and your friends going to do tomorrow afternoon?

What are YOU going to do tomorrow?

When Are You Going to . . .?

	Time Expressions	
this ____ next ____	week / month / year Sunday / Monday / Tuesday / Wednesday / Thursday / Friday / Saturday January / February / March / April / May / June / July / August / September / October / November / December spring / summer / fall (autumn) / winter	right now right away immediately at once

When are you going to wash your clothes?
I'm going to wash them this week.

When are you going to fix our doorbell?
I'm going to fix it next Friday.
5

When are you going to cut your hair?
I'm going to cut it this summer.

When are you going to call the plumber?
I'm going to call him right now.

Practice conversations with other students. Use any of the time expressions on page 130.

1. When are you going to clean your garage?

2. When are you going to call your grandmother?

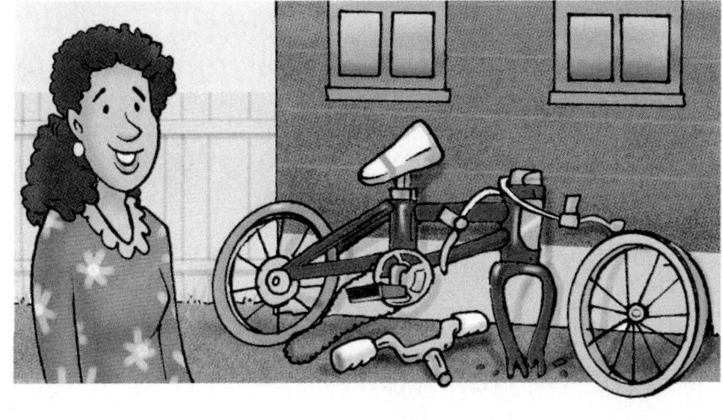

3. When are you going to fix your bicycle?

4. When are you going to visit us?

5. When are you going to wash your car?

6. When are you going to plant flowers this year?

7. When are you going to write to your Aunt Martha?

8. Mr. Smith! When are you going to iron those pants?

Now ask another student: "When are you going to ______?"

READING

HAPPY NEW YEAR!

It's December thirty-first, New Year's Eve. Ruth and Larry Carter are celebrating the holiday with their children, Nicole and Jonathan. The Carters are a very happy family this New Year's Eve. Next year is going to be a very good year for the entire family.

Next year, Ruth and Larry are going to take a long vacation. They're going to visit Larry's brother in Alaska. Nicole is going to finish high school. She's going to move to San Francisco and begin college. Jonathan is going to get his driver's license. He's going to save a lot of money and buy a used car.

As you can see, the Carters are really looking forward to next year. It's going to be a very happy year for all of them.

Happy New Year!

✓ READING *CHECK-UP*

COMPUTER CHAT

Fill in the missing words. Then practice this computer chat with another student.

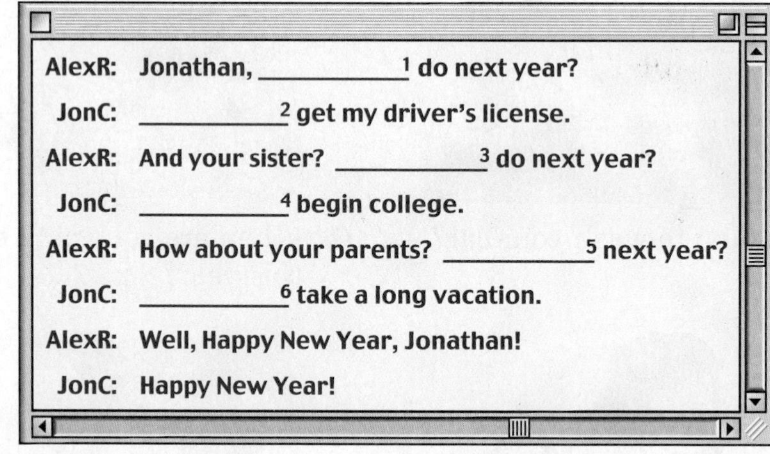

AlexR: Jonathan, __________1 do next year?

JonC: __________2 get my driver's license.

AlexR: And your sister? __________3 do next year?

JonC: __________4 begin college.

AlexR: How about your parents? __________5 next year?

JonC: __________6 take a long vacation.

AlexR: Well, Happy New Year, Jonathan!

JonC: Happy New Year!

LISTENING

Listen and choose the words you hear.

1.	a. Tomorrow.	b. This March.		
2.	a. Next December.	b. Next November.		
3.	a. Next month.	b. Next Monday.		
4.	a. This evening.	b. This morning.		
5.	a. This summer.	b. This Sunday.		
6.	a. This Tuesday.	b. This Thursday.		
7.	a. This afternoon.	b. Tomorrow afternoon.		
8.	a. Next year.	b. Next week.		
9.	a. Next winter.	b. Next summer.		
10.	a. This month.	b. At once.		

What's the Forecast?

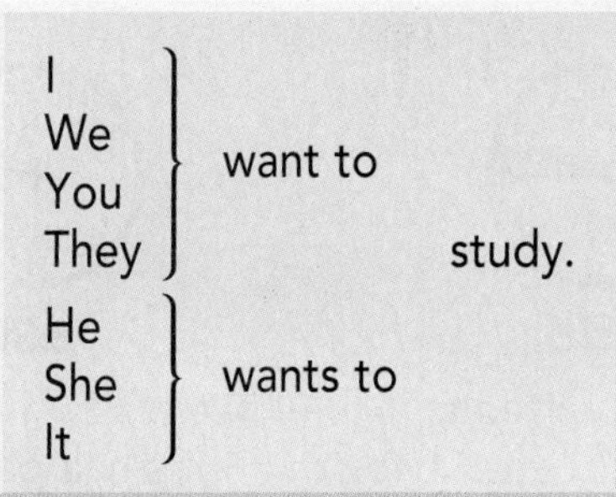

I We You They	want to	study.
He She It	wants to	

A. What are you going to do tomorrow?

B. I don't know. I want to **go swimming**, but I think the weather is going to be bad.

A. Really? What's the forecast?

B. The radio says it's going to **rain**.

A. That's strange! According to the newspaper, it's going to **be sunny**.

B. I hope you're right. I REALLY want to **go swimming**.

1. *have a picnic*
rain
be nice

2. *go to the beach*
be cloudy
be sunny

3. *go sailing*
be foggy
be clear

4. *go skiing*
be warm
snow

5. *work in my garden*
be very hot
be cool

6. *take my children to the zoo*
be cold
be warm

Discuss in class: What's the weather today? What's the weather forecast for tomorrow?

What Time Is It?

2:00
It's two o'clock.

2:15
It's two fifteen.
It's a quarter after two.

2:30
It's two thirty.
It's half past two.

2:45
It's two forty-five.
It's a quarter to three.

It's noon.
It's twelve noon.

It's midnight.
It's twelve midnight.

A. What time does the movie begin?

B. It begins at 8:00.

A. At 8:00?! Oh no! We're going to be late!

B. Why? What time is it?

A. It's 7:30! We have to leave RIGHT NOW!

B. I can't leave now. I'm SHAVING!

A. Please try to hurry! I don't want to be late for the movie.

A. What time does ______________________?

B. It __________ at __________.

A. At __________?! Oh no! We're going to be late!

B. Why? What time is it?

A. It's __________! We have to leave RIGHT NOW!

B. I can't leave now. I'm __________!

A. Please try to hurry! I don't want to be late for the __________.

1. What time does the football game begin?
3:00 / 2:30
taking a bath

2. What time does the bus leave?
7:15 / 6:45
packing my suitcase

3. What time does the train leave?
5:30 / 5:15
taking a shower

4. What time does the concert begin?
8:00 / 7:45
looking for my pants

How to Say It!

Asking the Time

A. { What time is it? / What's the time?

B. It's 4:00.

A. { Can you tell me the time? / Do you know the time?

B. Yes. It's 4:00.

Practice conversations with other students. Ask the time in different ways.

READING

THE FORTUNE TELLER

Walter is visiting Madame Sophia, the famous fortune teller. He's wondering about his future, and Madame Sophia is telling him what is going to happen next year. According to Madame Sophia, next year is going to be a very interesting year in Walter's life.

In January he's going to meet a very nice woman and fall in love.

In February he's going to get married.

In March he's going to take a trip to a warm, sunny place.

In April he's going to have a bad cold.

In May his parents are going to move to a beautiful city in California.

In June there's going to be a fire in his apartment building, and he's going to have to find a new place to live.

In July his friends are going to give him a DVD player for his birthday.

In August his boss is going to fire him.

In September he's going to start a new job with a very big salary.

In October he's going to be in a car accident, but he isn't going to be hurt.

In November he's going to be on a television game show and win a million dollars.

And in December he's going to become a father!

According to Madame Sophia, a lot is going to happen in Walter's life next year. But Walter isn't sure he believes any of this. He doesn't believe in fortunes or fortune tellers. But in January he's going to get a haircut and buy a lot of new clothes, just in case Madame Sophia is right and he meets a wonderful woman and falls in love!

✓ READING *CHECK-UP*

Q & A

Walter is talking to Madame Sophia. Using these models, create dialogs based on the story.

A. Tell me, what's going to happen in *January*?
B. In *January*? Oh! *January* is going to be a very good month!
A. Really? What's going to happen?
B. *You're going to meet a very nice woman and fall in love.*
A. Oh! That's wonderful!

A. Tell me, what's going to happen in *April*?
B. In *April*? Oh! *April* is going to be a very bad month!
A. Really? What's going to happen?
B. *You're going to have a bad cold.*
A. Oh! That's terrible!

PRONUNCIATION *Going to & Want to*

going to = gonna
want to = wanna

Listen. Then say it.

I'm going to study.

It's going to rain.

We want to go swimming.

They want to leave.

Say it. Then listen.

He's going to cook.

They're going to paint.

I want to read.

We want to go to the beach.

What are you going to do tomorrow? Write about it in your journal.

GRAMMAR FOCUS

Future: Going To

What	am	I	going to do?
	is	he she it	
	are	we you they	

(I am)	I'm	going to read.
(He is) (She is) (It is)	He's She's It's	
(We are) (You are) (They are)	We're You're They're	

Complete the sentences using *going to* and the correct verb.

go	read	wash	watch	write

1. A. What's your husband going to do this afternoon?
   B. _____ _____ _____ _____ a book.
2. A. What are you going to do this morning?
   B. _____ _____ _____ _____ a letter to my aunt.
3. A. What are Sally and Paul going to do tonight?
   B. _____ _____ _____ _____ TV.
4. A. What are you and your wife going to do this Saturday?
   B. _____ _____ _____ _____ our windows.
5. A. What's your sister going to do this Sunday?
   B. _____ _____ _____ _____ to the beach.

Time Expressions

I'm going to call	today. this morning. this afternoon. this evening. tonight.	tomorrow. tomorrow morning. tomorrow afternoon. tomorrow evening. tomorrow night.	right now. right away. immediately. at once.

I'm going to fix my car	this next	week / month / year. Sunday / Monday / Tuesday / . . . / Saturday. January / February / March / . . . / December. spring / summer / fall (autumn) / winter.

Number the following from the present (1) to the future (12).

____ next Saturday
____ tomorrow afternoon
____ next year
____ this Friday
__1__ immediately
____ this Wednesday
____ next month
____ tomorrow night
____ tonight
____ this evening
____ next Tuesday
____ this afternoon

It's	eleven o'clock.		11:00
	eleven fifteen.	a quarter after eleven.	11:15
	eleven thirty.	half past eleven.	11:30
	eleven forty-five.	a quarter to twelve.	11:45

Match the times.

____ 1. 3:15 — a. three forty-five
____ 2. 2:45 — b. half past two
____ 3. 2:30 — c. a quarter after three
____ 4. 3:45 — d. a quarter to three

Want To

I We You They	want to	study.
He She It	wants to	

Choose the correct word.

1. I (want to wants to) go to a movie tomorrow night.
2. My husband (want to wants to) go to the beach tomorrow.
3. My sister and I (want to wants to) go swimming today.
4. My parents (want to wants to) buy a new car.
5. Do you (want to wants to) have a picnic this afternoon?
6. My grandmother (want to wants to) work in her garden today.

SIDE by SIDE Gazette

Volume 1 Number 6

Time Zones

What time is it right now? What time is it in other parts of the world? How do you know?

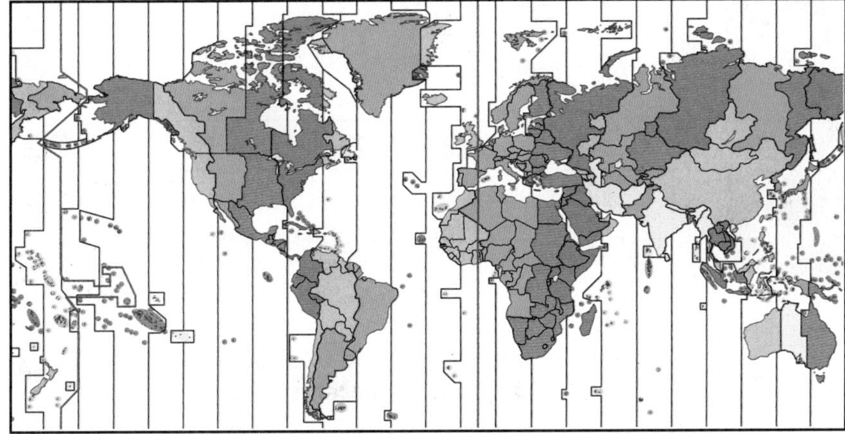

There are 24 time zones around the world. In each time zone, it is a different hour of the day. The time zone that is east of your time zone is one hour ahead. The time zone to your west is one hour behind. So, for example, when it's 10:00 in Chicago, it's 11:00 in New York, it's 9:00 in Denver, and it's 8:00 in Los Angeles.

New Zealand is 12 time zones to the east of London. Therefore, when it's midnight in London and people are sleeping, it's noon the next day in New Zealand and people are eating lunch!

FACT FILE

A Moment in the Life of the World

Time and Day		Place
5:00 A.M.*	Monday morning	Los Angeles, USA
7:00 A.M.	Monday morning	Mexico City, Mexico
8:00 A.M.	Monday morning	New York City, USA; Toronto, Canada
9:00 A.M.	Monday morning	Caracas, Venezuela
10:00 A.M.	Monday morning	Rio de Janeiro, Brazil; Buenos Aires, Argentina
1:00 P.M.*	Monday afternoon	London, England; Lisbon, Portugal
2:00 P.M.	Monday afternoon	Paris, France; Madrid, Spain; Rome, Italy
3:00 P.M.	Monday afternoon	Athens, Greece; Istanbul, Turkey
4:00 P.M.	Monday afternoon	Moscow, Russia
9:00 P.M.	Monday night	Hong Kong, China
10:00 P.M.	Monday night	Seoul, Korea; Tokyo, Japan
12:00 A.M.	Tuesday morning	Sydney, Australia

*A.M. = 12:00 midnight to 11:59 in the morning P.M. = 12:00 noon to 11:59 at night

BUILD YOUR VOCABULARY!

Occupations

A. What do you do?
B. I'm a/an ________ .

■ architect

■ carpenter

■ cashier

■ farmer

■ lawyer

■ painter

■ pilot

■ translator

■ waiter

■ waitress

AROUND THE WORLD

Time and Culture

People in different cultures think of time in different ways.

In your culture, do people arrive on time for work? Do people arrive on time for appointments? Do people arrive on time for parties? Tell about time in your culture.

LISTENING

Thank You for Calling the Multiplex Cinema!

c	1	a. *The Fortune Teller*
___	2	b. *Tomorrow Is Right Now*
___	3	c. *The Spanish Dancer*
___	4	d. *The Time Zone Machine*
___	5	e. *When Are You Going to Call the Plumber?*

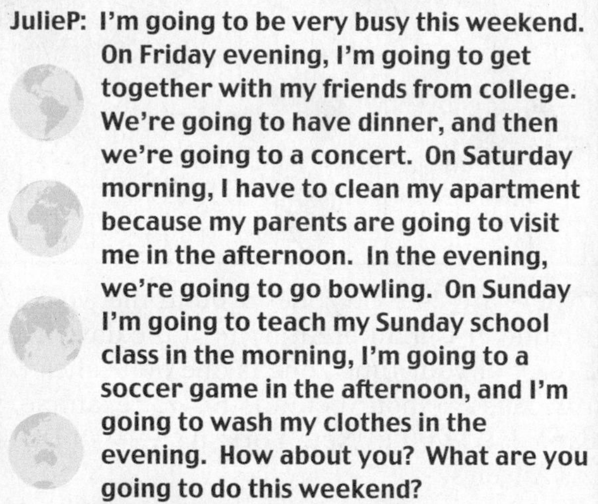

Global Exchange

JulieP: I'm going to be very busy this weekend. On Friday evening, I'm going to get together with my friends from college. We're going to have dinner, and then we're going to a concert. On Saturday morning, I have to clean my apartment because my parents are going to visit me in the afternoon. In the evening, we're going to go bowling. On Sunday I'm going to teach my Sunday school class in the morning, I'm going to a soccer game in the afternoon, and I'm going to wash my clothes in the evening. How about you? What are you going to do this weekend?

Send a message to a keypal. Tell about your plans for the weekend.

What Are They Saying?

15

Past Tense:
Regular Verbs
Introduction to Irregular Verbs

- Past Actions and Activities
- Ailments
- Describing an Event
- Making a Doctor's Appointment

Vocabulary Preview

1. headache
2. stomachache
3. toothache
4. backache
5. earache
6. cold
7. fever
8. cough
9. sore throat

How Do You Feel Today?

A. How do you feel today?

B. Not so good.

A. What's the matter?

B. I have a headache.

A. I'm sorry to hear that.

1. *stomachache*

2. *toothache*

3. *backache*

4. *earache*

5. *cold*

6. *fever*

7. *cough*

8. *sore throat*

How to Say It!

Saying How You Feel

Practice conversations with other students.

What Did You Do Yesterday?

t

I work every day.
I **worked** yesterday.

d

I play the piano every day.
I **played** the piano yesterday.

Id

I rest every day.
I **rested** yesterday.

What did you do yesterday?
I worked.

1. *cook*

2. *wash my car*

t

3. *fix my bicycle*

4. *brush my teeth*

5. *watch TV*

6. *type**

7. *dance**

8. *bake**

9. *clean*

d

10. *play the piano*

11. *yawn*

12. *listen to music*

13. *shave**

14. *smile**

15. *cry*†

16. *study*†

17. *shout*

18. *rest*

Id

19. *plant flowers*

20. *wait for the bus*

* type – typed
dance – danced
bake – baked

shave – shaved
smile – smiled

† cry – cried
study – studied

What's the Matter?

I We You They	work every day.
He She It	works every day.

I We You They He She It	worked yesterday.

A. How does David feel?

B. Not so good.

A. What's the matter?

B. He has a backache.

A. A backache? How did he get it?

B. He played basketball all day.*

* Or: all morning/all afternoon/all evening/all night

1. *Brian*

2. *Linda*

3. *you*

4. *Gary*

5. *Maria*

6. *Charlie*

7. *Mrs. Clark*

8. *you*

9. *Carlos*

eat – ate	sing – sang	drink – drank	sit – sat	ride – rode

10. *Daniel*

11. *Jennifer*

12. *you*

13. *Sarah*

14. *you*

15. *Tim*

ROLE PLAY *Do You Want to Make an Appointment?*

You don't feel very well today. Call the doctor's office and make an appointment.

A. Doctor's Office.

B. Hello. This is ______________.

A. Hello, Mr./Ms./Mrs. __________.
How are you?

B. Not so good.

A. I'm sorry to hear that. What seems to be the problem?

B. I __________ all __________ yesterday, and now I have a TERRIBLE __________.

A. I see. Do you want to make an appointment?

B. Yes, please.

A. Can you come in tomorrow at ________ o'clock?

B. At ________ o'clock? Yes. That's fine. Thank you.

THE WILSONS' PARTY

Mr. and Mrs. Wilson invited all their friends and neighbors to a party last night. They stayed home all day yesterday and prepared for the party.

In the morning the Wilsons worked outside. Their daughter, Margaret, cleaned the yard. Their son, Bob, painted the fence. Mrs. Wilson planted flowers in the garden, and Mr. Wilson fixed their broken front steps.

In the afternoon the Wilsons worked inside the house. Margaret washed the floors and vacuumed the living room carpet. Bob dusted the furniture and cleaned the basement. Mr. and Mrs. Wilson stayed in the kitchen all afternoon. He cooked spaghetti for dinner, and she baked apple pies for dessert.

The Wilsons finished all their work at six o'clock. Their house looked beautiful inside and out!

The Wilsons' guests arrived at about 7:30. After they arrived, they all sat in the living room. They ate cheese and crackers, drank lemonade, and talked. Some people talked about their children. Other people talked about the weather. And EVERYBODY talked about how beautiful the Wilsons' house looked inside and out!

The Wilsons served dinner in the dining room at 9:00. Everybody enjoyed the meal very much. They liked Mr. Wilson's spaghetti and they "loved" Mrs. Wilson's apple pie. In fact, everybody asked for seconds.

After dinner everybody sat in the living room again. First, Bob Wilson played the piano and his sister, Margaret, sang. Then, Mr. and Mrs. Wilson showed a video of their trip to Hawaii. After that, they turned on the music and everybody danced.

As you can see, the Wilsons' guests enjoyed the party very much. In fact, nobody wanted to go home!

✓ READING *CHECK-UP*

WHAT'S THE ANSWER?

1. What did Margaret and Bob Wilson do in the morning?
2. How did Mr. and Mrs. Wilson prepare for the party in the afternoon?
3. When did the guests arrive?
4. Where did the guests sit after they arrived?
5. What did they eat and drink before dinner?
6. What did Margaret do after dinner?
7. What did Mr. and Mrs. Wilson do after dinner?

LISTENING

Listen and choose the word you hear.

1. a. plant b. planted
2. a. work b. worked
3. a. study b. studied
4. a. sit b. sat
5. a. drink b. drank
6. a. wait b. waited
7. a. finish b. finished
8. a. invite b. invited
9. a. eat b. ate
10. a. clean b. cleaned
11. a. wash b. washed
12. a. watch b. watched

IN YOUR OWN WORDS

FOR WRITING OR DISCUSSION

A PARTY

Tell about a party you enjoyed.

What did you eat?
What did you drink?
What did people do at the party?
(eat, dance, talk about . . .)

PRONUNCIATION *Past Tense Endings*

Put these words in the correct column. Then practice saying the words in each column.

cleaned	danced	dusted	painted	played	studied	talked	typed	waited

[t]	[d]	[ɪd]
________	cleaned	________
________	________	________
________	________	________

Listen. Then say it.

I cooked, I cleaned, and I dusted.

I worked, I played, and I planted flowers.

Say it. Then listen.

I typed, I studied, and I painted.

I talked, I cried, and I shouted.

What did you eat yesterday?
What did you drink?
Write about it in your journal.

GRAMMAR FOCUS

PAST TENSE

I He She It We You They	worked yesterday.

[t]	I worked. I danced.
[d]	I cleaned. I played.
[ɪd]	I rested. I shouted.

IRREGULAR VERBS

eat	ate
drink	drank
ride	rode
sing	sang
sit	sat

Complete each sentence with the past tense of the correct verb.

drink	listen	play	sing	study	wash
eat	plant	ride	sit	wait	watch

1. I ________ my car yesterday.
2. I ________ TV yesterday.
3. I ________ the piano yesterday.
4. I ________ to music yesterday.
5. I ________ flowers yesterday.
6. I ________ English yesterday.
7. I ________ four cookies this afternoon.
8. I ________ milk with my lunch today.
9. I have a sore throat because I ________ all day yesterday.
10. My daughter ________ her bicycle all afternoon.
11. I ________ at my desk all day yesterday.
12. I ________ for the bus all morning.

16

Past Tense:

Yes/No Questions
Short Answers
WH-Questions
More Irregular Verbs
Time Expressions

- Reporting Past Actions and Activities
- Giving Reasons
- Giving Excuses

Vocabulary Preview

1. got up
2. took a shower
3. had breakfast
4. read the newspaper
5. did exercises
6. ate lunch
7. drove to the supermarket
8. bought groceries
9. made dinner
10. wrote a letter
11. saw a movie
12. went to sleep

I Brushed My Teeth

I worked. I didn't work. (did not)	Did you work? Yes, I did. No, I didn't.

today	*yesterday*
this morning	yesterday morning
this afternoon	yesterday afternoon
this evening	yesterday evening
tonight	last night

Did you brush your hair this morning?
No, I didn't. I brushed my teeth.

1. Did he wash his windows yesterday morning?

2. Did she paint her kitchen this afternoon?

3. Did they study English last night?

4. Did you and your friends play tennis yesterday afternoon?

5. Did he bake a pie today?

6. Did you listen to the news this morning?

We Went to the Supermarket

I went.
I didn't go.
(did not)

Did you go?
Yes, I did.
No, I didn't.

Did you go to the bank this afternoon?
No, we didn't. We went to the supermarket.

go
went

take
took

1. Did you take the subway this morning?

have
had

2. Did he have a headache last night?

7:00

get
got

3. Did Wanda get up at 9:00 this morning?

make
made

4. Did your children make dinner today?

buy
bought

5. Did Michael buy a car yesterday?

do
did

6. Did they do their homework last night?

Dear Grandmother,

write
wrote

7. Did Tommy write to his girlfriend this week?

read
read

8. Did you read the newspaper this afternoon?

TALK ABOUT IT! *What Did They Do Yesterday?*

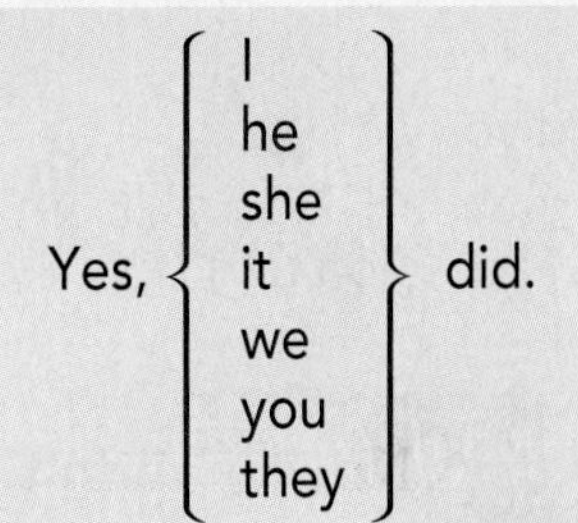
Yes, { I / he / she / it / we / you / they } did.

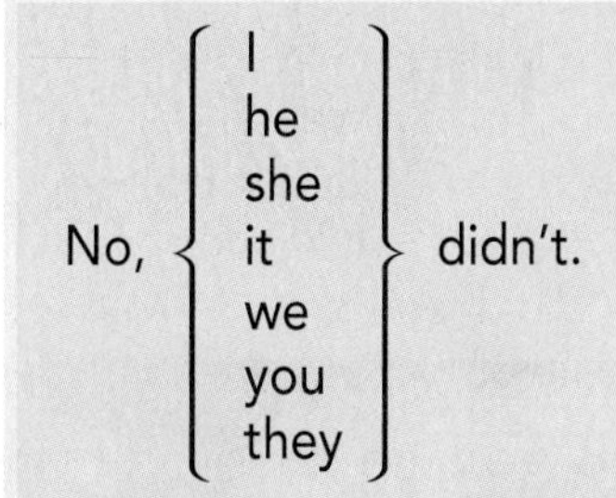
No, { I / he / she / it / we / you / they } didn't.

Betty fixed her car yesterday morning.
She washed her windows yesterday afternoon.
She listened to music last night.

Bob read the newspaper yesterday morning.
He went to the library yesterday afternoon.
He wrote letters last night.

Nick and Nancy went to the supermarket yesterday morning.
They bought a new car yesterday afternoon.
They cleaned their apartment last night.

Jennifer did her exercises yesterday morning.
She planted flowers yesterday afternoon.
She took a bath last night.

Using these models, talk about the people above with other students in your class.

A. Did *Betty fix her car yesterday morning?*
B. Yes, *she* did.

A. Did *Bob go to the library last night?*
B. No, *he* didn't. *He went to the library yesterday afternoon.*

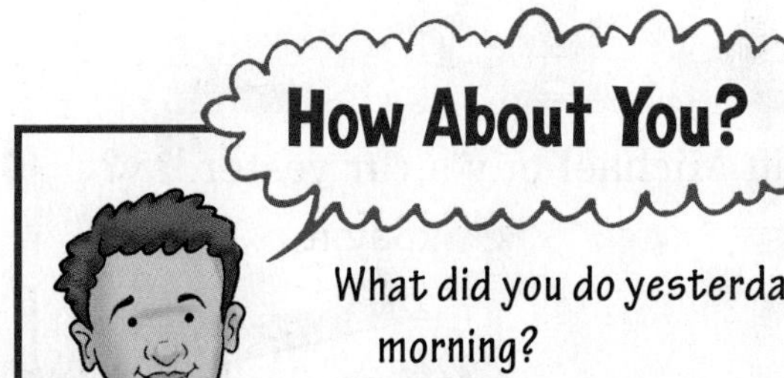

How About You?
What did you do yesterday morning?
What did you do yesterday afternoon?
What did you do last night?

How to Say It!

Giving an Excuse

A. I'm sorry I'm late. *I missed the bus.*
B. I see.

Practice the interactions on this page. Apologize and give excuses.

INTERACTIONS

A. I'm sorry I'm late. ________________.
B. I see.

I missed the ______.
(bus / train . . .)

I had a _____ this morning.
(headache / stomachache / . . .)

I had to go to the ______.
(doctor / dentist / . . .)

I forgot* my _____ and had to go back home and get it.
(briefcase / backpack / . . .)

A thief stole* my ______.
(bicycle / car / . . .)

THINK ABOUT IT! *Good Excuses & Bad Excuses*

The people above have good excuses. Here are some BAD excuses:

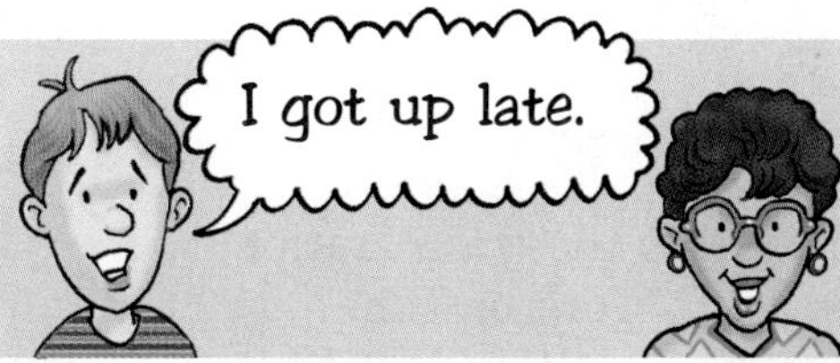

I got up late.
I had a big breakfast today.
I met* a friend on the way to work/school.

Discuss with other students: What are some good excuses? What are some bad excuses? Why are these excuses good or bad?

* forget – forgot steal – stole meet – met

READING

LATE FOR WORK

Victor usually gets up at 7 A.M. He does his morning exercises for twenty minutes, he takes a long shower, he has a big breakfast, and he leaves for work at 8:00. He usually drives his car to work and gets there at 8:30.

This morning, however, he didn't get up at 7 A.M. He got up at 6:30. He didn't do his morning exercises for twenty minutes. He did them for only five minutes. He didn't take a long shower. He took a very quick shower. He didn't have a big breakfast. He had a very small breakfast. He didn't leave for work at 8:00. He left for work at 7:00.

Victor didn't drive his car to work this morning. He drove it to the repair shop. Then he walked a mile to the train station, and he waited for the train for fifteen minutes. After he got off the train, he walked half a mile to his office.

Even though Victor got up early and rushed out of the house this morning, he didn't get to work on time. He got there forty-five minutes late. When his supervisor saw him, she got angry and she shouted at him for five minutes. Poor Victor! He really tried to get to work on time this morning.

✓ READING *CHECK-UP*

WHAT'S THE ANSWER?

1. Did Victor get up at 7 A.M. today?
2. What time did he get up?
3. Did he leave for work at 8:00 this morning?
4. What time did he leave for work?
5. Did he drive his car to the repair shop today?
6. How did he get to the train station?
7. Did Victor get to work on time?
8. Did his supervisor get angry at him?
9. What did she do?

WHICH IS CORRECT?

1. Victor (got up didn't get up) at 6:30 A.M. this morning.
2. He (did didn't do) his exercises for twenty minutes today.
3. He (took didn't take) a very quick shower this morning.
4. He (left didn't leave) for work at 8:00 this morning.
5. He (took didn't take) the train to work today.
6. He (got didn't get) to work on time this morning.

LISTENING

Listen and put a check next to all the things these people did today.

Carla's Day

___ got up early
___ got up late
___ took a bath
___ took a shower
___ had breakfast
___ had lunch
___ took the subway
___ took the bus
___ met her brother
___ met her mother
___ had dinner
___ made dinner
___ saw a movie
___ saw a play

Brian's Day

___ fixed his car
___ fixed his bicycle
___ cleaned his garage
___ cleaned his yard
___ painted his bedroom
___ planted flowers
___ washed his windows
___ watched TV
___ read the newspaper
___ read a magazine
___ rode his bicycle
___ wrote to his brother
___ took a shower
___ took a bath

COMPLETE THE STORY

Complete the story with the correct forms of the verbs.

buy eat get go make see sit take

SHIRLEY'S DAY OFF

Shirley enjoyed her day off yesterday. She ________1 up late, ________2 jogging in the park, ________3 a long shower, and ________4 a big breakfast. In the afternoon, she ________5 a movie with her sister. Then she ________6 groceries at the supermarket, and she ________7 a big dinner for her parents. After dinner, Shirley and her parents ________8 in the living room and talked. Shirley had a very nice day off yesterday.

How About You?
Tell about a day off YOU enjoyed. What did you do in the morning? in the afternoon? in the evening?

PRONUNCIATION *Did you*

Listen. Then say it.

Did you go to the bank?

Did you brush your hair?

Did you listen to the news?

Did you take the subway?

Say it. Then listen.

Did you go to the supermarket?

Did you play tennis?

Did you read the newspaper?

Did you see a movie?

What did you do yesterday? Write in your journal about all the things you did.

GRAMMAR FOCUS

Past Tense: Yes/No Questions

Did	I he she it we you they	work?

Short Answers

Yes,	I he she it we you they	did.

No,	I he she it we you they	didn't.

Past Tense: WH-Questions

What did	I he she it we you they	do?

Time Expressions

Did you study English	yesterday? yesterday morning? yesterday afternoon? yesterday evening? last night?

Complete the conversations with the correct forms of these verbs.

do	go	have	listen	study	take	wash	watch

1. A. Did you _______ the bus this morning?
B. No, I didn't. I _______ the train.

2. A. Did your children _______ last night?
B. Yes, they did. They _______ English.

3. A. Did you _______ your windows yesterday?
B. No, we didn't. We _______ our car.

4. A. Did you _______ to the bank this morning?
B. No, I didn't. I _______ to the post office.

5. A. Did you _______ a stomachache yesterday?
B. Yes, I _______. I also _______ a headache.

6. A. _______ Stella _______ TV last night?
B. No, she didn't. She _______ to music.

17

To Be: Past Tense

- Television Commercials
- Describing Physical States and Emotions
- Telling About the Past
- Biographies and Autobiographies

Vocabulary Preview

1  

2 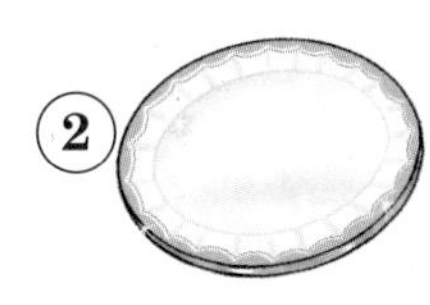 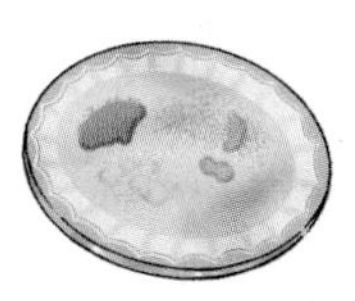

3  

4  

5 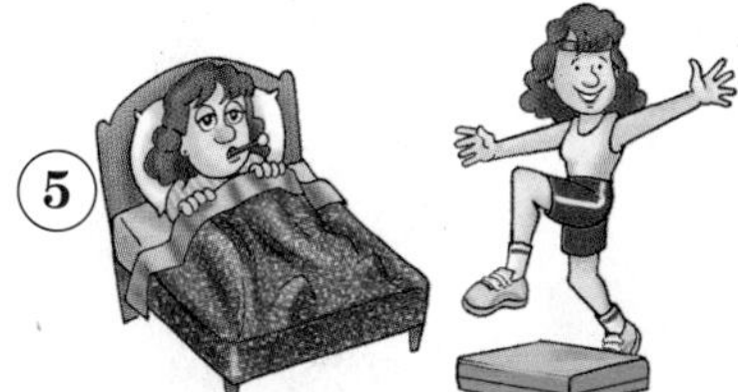

6 

7  

8 

9 

1. sad – happy
2. clean – dirty
3. heavy – thin
4. hungry – full
5. sick – healthy
6. tiny – enormous
7. dull – shiny
8. comfortable – uncomfortable
9. tired – energetic

PRESTO Commercials

I He She It	was	happy.
We You They	were	

Before our family bought PRESTO Vitamins, we were always tired.
I was tired.
My wife was tired.
My children were tired, too.
Now we're energetic, because WE bought PRESTO Vitamins. How about you?

Before our family bought __________, we were always __________.

I was __________.

My wife/husband was __________.

My children were __________, too.

Now we're __________ because WE bought __________. How about you?

Using the above script, prepare commercials for these other fine PRESTO products.

1. *sad* *happy*

2. *hungry* *full*

3. *dirty* *clean*

4. *sick* *healthy*

5. *heavy* *thin*

6. ________ ________

Before I Bought PRESTO Shampoo

Before I bought PRESTO Shampoo, my hair **was** always dirty. Now **it's** clean!

1. Before we bought PRESTO Toothpaste, our teeth _______ yellow. Now _______ white!

2. Before we bought PRESTO Paint, our house _______ ugly. Now _______ beautiful!

3. Before I bought a PRESTO armchair, I _______ uncomfortable. Now _______ very comfortable!

4. Before we bought PRESTO Dog Food, our dog _______ tiny. Now _______ enormous!

5. Before I bought PRESTO Window Cleaner, my windows _______ dirty. Now _______ clean!

6. Before we bought PRESTO Floor Wax, our kitchen floor _______ dull. Now _______ shiny!

How to Say It!

Recommending Products

A. Can you recommend a good *toothpaste*?

B. Yes. I recommend *PRESTO Toothpaste*. It's very good.

A. Thanks for the recommendation.

Practice conversations with other students. Make recommendations about real products.

Were You at the Ballgame Last Night?

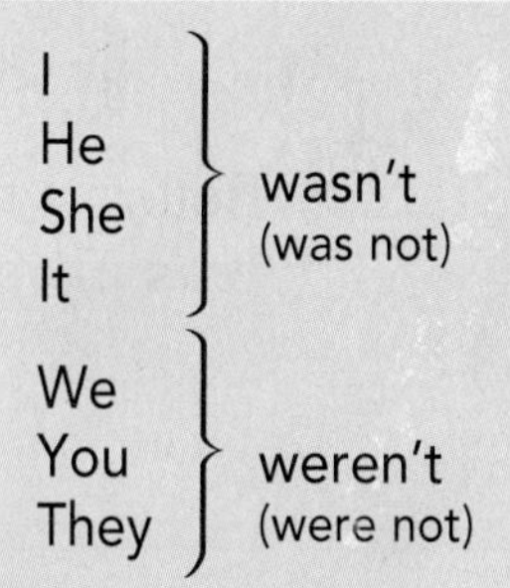

I He She It	wasn't (was not)
We You They	weren't (were not)

A. Were you at the ballgame last night?

B. No, I wasn't. I was at the movies.

1. Was Albert happy yesterday?

2. Were they at home this morning?

3. Was it cold yesterday?

4. Was your grandfather a doctor?

5. Was I a quiet baby?

6. Were you at home last weekend?

7. Was Gloria on time for her plane?

8. Were your children late for the school bus?

9. Was the food good at the restaurant?

Did You Sleep Well Last Night?

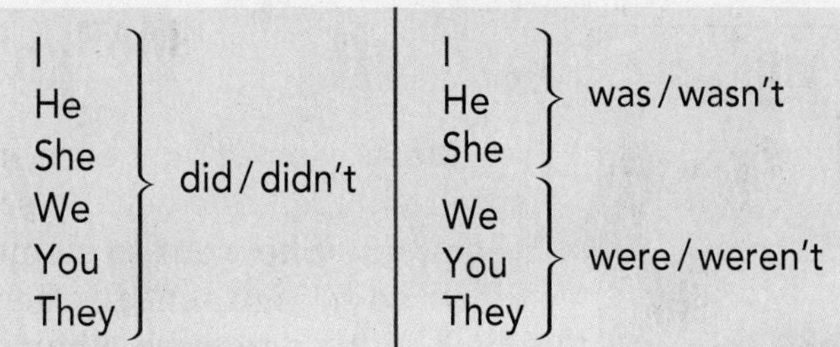

I, He, She, We, You, They	did / didn't	I, He, She	was / wasn't
		We, You, They	were / weren't

A. Did you sleep well last night?
B. Yes, I did. I was tired.

A. Did Roger sleep well last night?
B. No, he didn't. He wasn't tired.

1. Did Frank have a big breakfast today?
Yes, ______. ____________ *hungry.*

2. Did Thelma have a big breakfast today?
No, ______. ____________ *hungry.*

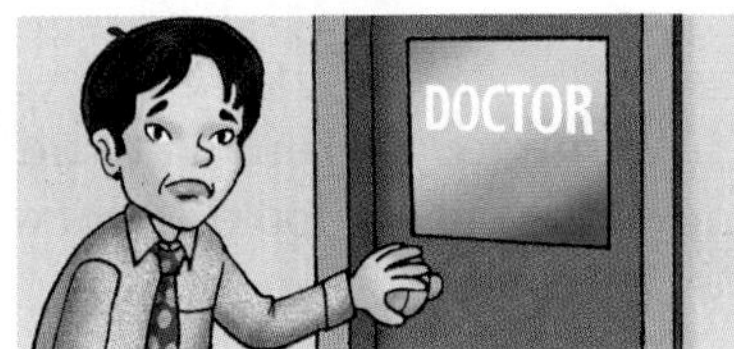

3. Did Mr. Chen go to the doctor yesterday?
Yes, ______. ____________ *sick.*

4. Did Mrs. Chen go to the doctor yesterday?
No, ______. ____________ *sick.*

5. Did Billy finish his milk?
Yes, ______. ____________ *thirsty.*

6. Did Katie finish her milk?
No, ______. ____________ *thirsty.*

7. Did Sonia miss the train?
Yes, ______. ____________ *late.*

8. Did Stuart miss the train?
No , ______. ____________ *late.*

READING

MARIA GOMEZ

Maria Gomez was born in Peru. She grew* up in a small village. She began* school when she was six years old. She went to elementary school, but she didn't go to high school. Her family was very poor, and she had to go to work when she was thirteen years old. She worked on an assembly line in a shoe factory.

When Maria was seventeen years old, her family moved to the United States. First they lived in Los Angeles, and then they moved to San Francisco. When Maria arrived in the United States, she wasn't very happy. She missed her friends back in Peru, and she didn't speak one word of English. She began to study English at night, and she worked in a factory during the day.

Maria studied very hard. She learned English, and she got a good job as a secretary. Maria still studies at night, but now she studies advertising at a business school. She wants to work for an advertising company some day and write commercials.

Maria still misses her friends back home, but she communicates with them very often over the Internet. She's very happy now, and she's looking forward to an exciting future.

✓ READING *CHECK-UP*

WHAT'S THE ANSWER?

1. Where was Maria born?
2. Did she grow up in a large city?
3. When did she begin school?
4. What happened when Maria was seventeen years old?
5. Why was Maria unhappy when she arrived in the United States?
6. What is Maria's occupation?
7. What does she want to do in the future?
8. How does Maria communicate with her friends back home?

* grow – grew begin – began

WHAT'S THE ORDER?

Put these sentences in the correct order based on the story.

____ Maria's family moved to the United States.
____ Maria studies advertising now.
_1_ Maria grew up in a small village.
____ Maria's family moved to San Francisco.
____ Maria worked in a shoe factory.
____ Maria began to study English at night.
____ Maria went to elementary school.
____ Maria's family lived in Los Angeles.
____ Maria got a job as a secretary.

LISTENING

Listen and choose the correct answer.

1. a. They were sick.
   b. They're sick now.
2. a. Their old chairs were comfortable.
   b. Their new chairs are comfortable.
3. a. Lucy was very thirsty.
   b. Lucy wasn't thirsty.
4. a. Fred was on time this morning.
   b. Fred wasn't on time this morning.
5. a. Peter and Mary were at work yesterday.
   b. Peter and Mary are at work today.
6. a. Their kitchen floor wasn't shiny.
   b. Their kitchen floor is dull now.

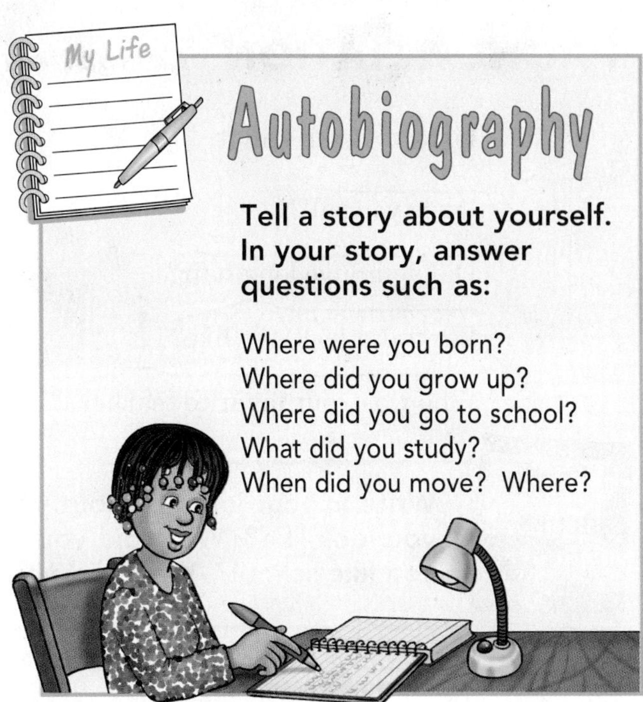

Autobiography

Tell a story about yourself. In your story, answer questions such as:

Where were you born?
Where did you grow up?
Where did you go to school?
What did you study?
When did you move? Where?

ON YOUR OWN *Do You Remember Your Childhood?*

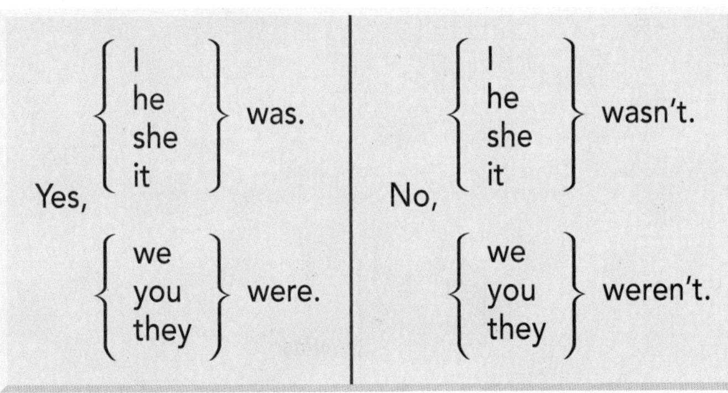

Yes,	No,
{I / he / she / it} was.	{I / he / she / it} wasn't.
{we / you / they} were.	{we / you / they} weren't.

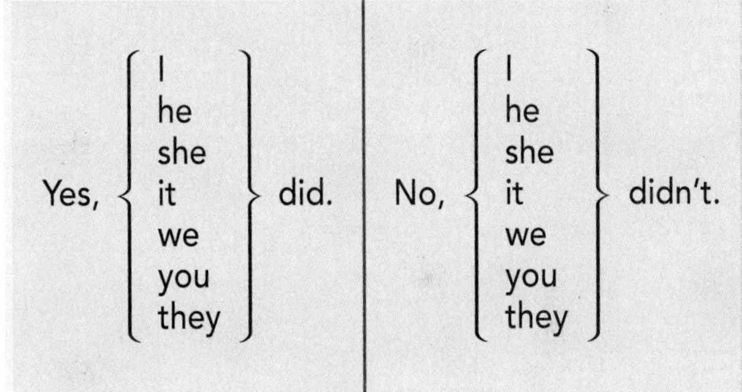

Yes,	No,
{I / he / she / it / we / you / they} did.	{I / he / she / it / we / you / they} didn't.

Answer these questions and then ask other students in your class.

1. What did you look like?
   Were you tall? thin? pretty? handsome? cute?
   Did you have curly hair? straight hair? long hair?
   Did you have dimples? freckles?
2. Did you have many friends?
   What did you do with your friends?
   What games did you play?
3. Did you like school?
   Who was your favorite teacher? Why?
   What was your favorite subject? Why?
4. What did you do in your spare time?
   Did you have a hobby?
   Did you play sports?
5. Who was your favorite hero?

PRONUNCIATION *Intonation of Yes/No Questions and WH-Questions*

Listen. Then say it.

Were you tall?

Did you have long hair?

What did you look like?

Who was your favorite teacher?

Say it. Then listen.

Were you short?

Did you have freckles?

Where did you grow up?

When did you move?

Write in your journal about your childhood. What did you look like? What did you do with your friends? Did you like school? What did you do in your spare time?

GRAMMAR FOCUS

To Be: Past Tense

I He She It	was	happy.
We You They	were	

I He She It	wasn't	tired.
We You They	weren't	

Was	I he she it	late?
Were	we you they	

Yes,	I he she it	was.
	we you they	were.

No,	I he she it	wasn't.
	we you they	weren't.

Complete the sentences.

1. A. ______ it hot yesterday?
B. Yes, it ______. It ______ very hot.

2. A. ______ you at home yesterday evening?
B. No, we ______. We ______ at the movies.

3. A. ______ George on time for work today?
B. No, he ______. He ______ late.

4. A. ______ your neighbors noisy last night?
B. Yes, they ______. They ______ very noisy all night.

5. A. ______ your wife at the ballgame last night?
B. Yes, ______ ______. She ______ next to me.

6. A. ______ you at work last night?
B. No, ______ ______. I ______ at the laundromat.

7. A. ______ your homework difficult today?
B. No, ______ ______. It ______ very easy.

8. A. ______ I a healthy baby?
B. Yes, ______ ______. You ______ a very healthy baby.

SIDE by SIDE Gazette

Volume 1 Number 7

Advertisements

How do advertisers sell their products?

Advertisements are everywhere! They are on television, on the radio, and in newspapers and magazines. Ads are also on billboards, on buses and trains, and even in movie theaters. People get advertisements in their mail. There are also a lot of advertisements on the Internet.

Advertisements are sometimes in unusual places—in elevators, on top of taxis, and in public bathrooms. People sometimes carry signs with ads on the street, and small airplanes sometimes carry signs in the sky. Advertisers are always looking for new places for their ads.

FACT FILE

Countries Where Advertisers Spend the Most Money

United States	Brazil
Japan	Italy
United Kingdom	Australia
Germany	Canada
France	Korea

LISTENING

And Now a Word From Our Sponsors!

d	1 Dazzle	a. floor wax
____	2 Shiny-Time	b. dog shampoo
____	3 Energy Plus	c. throat lozenges
____	4 Lucky Lemon Drops	d. toothpaste
____	5 K-9 Shine	e. vitamins

BUILD YOUR VOCABULARY!

Opposites

dark

light

fancy

plain

fast

slow

good

bad

heavy

light

high

low

long

short

neat

messy

open

closed

wet

dry

AROUND THE WORLD

Shopping

People around the world buy things in different ways.

This person is shopping in a store.

These people are buying things at an outdoor market.

This person is ordering something from a catalog over the telephone.

This person is buying something from a home shopping channel on TV.

These people are looking for things at a yard sale.

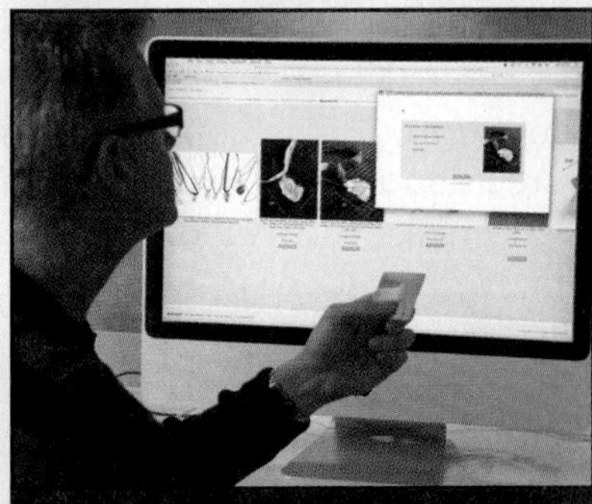

This person is shopping on the Internet.

What are the ways people buy things in different countries you know?

Global Exchange

TedG: I had a very busy day today. I got up at 6:30, took a shower, ate breakfast, and went to school. In my English class this morning, I read a long story, and I wrote my autobiography. I didn't have time for lunch because I had to meet with my Spanish teacher. After I met with her, I went to math class. We had a big test today. It was very difficult! After school, I went to a basketball game. Then I went home, did some homework, had dinner, and did some more homework. How about you? What did you do today?

Send a message to a keypal. Tell about what you did today.

What Are They Saying?

ACTIVITY WORKBOOK

Steven J. Molinsky

Bill Bliss

with

Carolyn Graham • Peter S. Bliss

Contributing Authors

Dorothy Lynde • Elizabeth Handley

Illustrated by

Richard E. Hill

CONTENTS

A INTERVIEWS AROUND THE WORLD

STUDENT BOOK PAGES **79–86**

what	language	we	our	is	eat	read
what's	name	you	your	are	live	watch
where	names	they	their	do	sing	speak

A. What's [1] your name?

B. My ________ [2] ________ [3] Sung Hee.

A. Where ________ [4] ________ [5] live?

B. I ________ [6] in Seoul.

A. ________ [7] ________ [8] do you speak?

B. I ________ [9] Korean.

A. What ________ [10] ________ [11] do every day?

B. Every day I ________ [12] Korean food, and I ________ [13] Korean TV shows.

A. What ________ [14] your names?

B. ________ [15] ________ [16] are Carlos and Maria.

A. Where ________ [17] ________ [18] live?

B. ________ [19] ________ [20] in Madrid.

A. ________ [21] language ________ [22] ________ [23] speak?

B. We ________ [24] Spanish.

A. What ________ [25] you ________ [26] every day?

B. Every day ________ [27] ________ [28] Spanish songs, and we ________ [29] Spanish newspapers.

A. ________30 ________31 their names?

B. ________32 ________33 ________34

Yuko and Toshi.

A. ________35 ________36 they live?

B. ________37 ________38 in Kyoto.

A. ________39 ________40 ________41

________42 speak?

B. They ________43 Japanese.

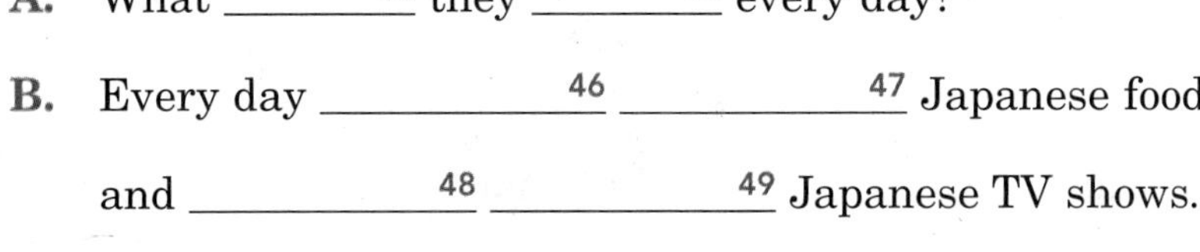

A. What ________44 they ________45 every day?

B. Every day ________46 ________47 Japanese food,

and ________48 ________49 Japanese TV shows.

B LISTENING

Listen and choose the correct response.

1. ⓐ My name is Kenji.
   b. I live in Tokyo.

2. a. They speak Italian.
   b. I speak Italian.

3. a. They watch Russian TV shows.
   b. I watch Russian TV shows.

4. a. We live in Seoul.
   b. They live in Seoul.

5. a. We eat French food.
   b. We speak French.

6. a. They live in Madrid.
   b. We sing Spanish songs.

C PEOPLE AROUND THE WORLD

My name is Jane. I live in Montreal. Every day I play the piano, and I listen to Canadian music.

1. What's her name? *Her name is Jane.*
2. Where does she live? ________________
3. What does she do every day? ________________

(continued)

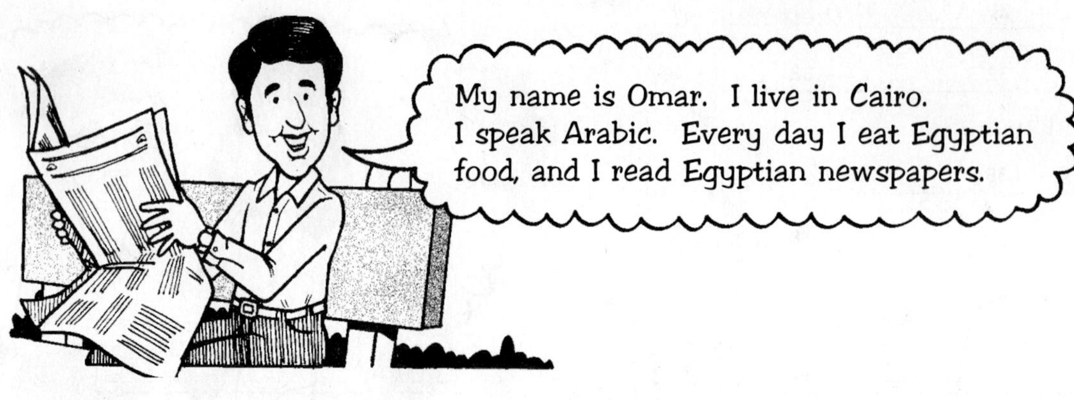

My name is Omar. I live in Cairo.
I speak Arabic. Every day I eat Egyptian food, and I read Egyptian newspapers.

4. ______________________________? His name is Omar.

5. ______________________________? He lives in Cairo.

6. What language does he speak? ______________________________

7. What ______________ every day? He __________ Egyptian food, and __________ ______________________________.

My name is Sonia. I live in Sao Paolo.
I speak Portuguese. Every day I do exercises, and I play soccer.

8. What's her name? ______________________________

9. ______________________________ she live? ______________________________

10. What language ______________________________? ______________________________

11. What ______________ every day? ______________________________ ______________________________

D WRITE ABOUT YOURSELF

1. What's your name? ....

2. Where do you live? ....

3. What language do you speak? ....

4. What do you do every day? ....

E GrammarRap: *People and Places*

Listen. Then clap and practice.

A. What's his name?
B. His name is Joe.
A. Where does he live?
B. In Mexico.

A. What's his name?
B. His name is Lance.
A. Where does he live?
B. He lives in France.

A. What's her name?
B. Her name is Anne.
A. Where does she live?
B. She lives in Japan.

A. What's her name?
B. Her name is Anastasia.
A. Where does she live?
B. She lives in Malaysia.

A. What's her name?
B. Her name is Denise.
A. Where does she live?
B. She lives in Greece.

A. What's her name?
B. Her name is Maria.
A. Where does she live?
B. She lives in Korea.

F EDUARDO'S FAMILY

Fill in the correct form of the verb.

clean	cook	do	live	play	read	shop	speak	work
cleans	cooks	does	lives	plays	reads	shops	speaks	works

My name is Eduardo. I ___live___ 1 in Rio de Janeiro. I __________ 2 English and Portuguese. My wife's name is Sonia. She __________ 3 English, Portuguese, and Spanish. Our children, Fernando and Claudio, also __________ 4 English and Portuguese. At school they __________ 5 English and Portuguese books.

We __________ 6 in a large apartment. Every day my wife __________ 7 the newspaper and __________ 8 in a bank. I __________ 9 breakfast and __________ 10 in an office.

Every weekend we __________ 11 our apartment. I also __________ 12 at the supermarket. Fernando __________ 13 soccer with his friends, and Claudio and I __________ 14 basketball.

What languages __________ 15 YOU speak? What do YOU __________ 16 every day?

G LISTENING 

Listen and circle the word you hear.

1.	(live)	lives	**4.**	listen	listens	**7.**	sing	sings
2.	do	does	**5.**	watch	watches	**8.**	eat	eats
3.	do	does	**6.**	eat	eats	**9.**	read	reads

H WHAT'S THE WORD?

do does	cook	drive	live	paint	sell

1. A. Where ___does___ he live?
   B. He ___lives___ in San Francisco.

2. A. What ______________ they do?
   B. They ______________ houses.

3. A. What ______________ he do?
   B. He ______________ a bus.

4. A. Where ______________ you live?
   B. I ______________ in Sydney.

5. A. What ______________ you do?
   B. We ______________ in a restaurant.

6. A. What ________ he ________?
   B. He ______________ cars.

I WHAT'S THE DIFFERENCE?

1. I drive a bus. My friend Carla ___drives___ a taxi.
2. We ____________ in a bank. They work in an office.
3. Victor ____________ the violin. His children play the piano.
4. I sell cars. My wife ____________ computers.
5. I paint houses. My brother ____________ pictures.
6. We live in Los Angeles. Our son ____________ in London.

J LISTEN AND PRONOUNCE

Listen to each word and then say it.

1. chair	4. Chen	7. church	10. children	13. Sharp	16. Shirley	19. short
2. bench	5. kitchen	8. cheap	11. Richard	14. shirt	17. washing	20. English
3. Charlie	6. Chinese	9. watch	12. shoes	15. machine	18. station	21. French

K LOUD AND CLEAR

Fill in the words. Then read the sentences aloud.

chair   Charlie   kitchen   Chinese

1. ___Charlie___ is sitting in a ___chair___ in his ________ and eating ________ food.

Shirley   short   shoes

2. ________ isn't ________ in her new ________.

watch   Richard   cheap   French

3. ________ is looking for a ________ ________ ________.

shirt   washing   washing machine

4. He's ________ his ________ in his ________ ________.

bench   children   Chen   church

5. Mr. ________ and his ________ are sitting on a ________ in front of the ________.

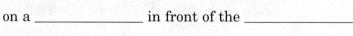

Sharp   station   English

6. Mr. ________ is in London at an ________ train ________.

A WHAT'S THE DAY?

1. Monday ___Tuesday___ Wednesday
2. Friday __________ Sunday
3. Tuesday __________ Thursday
4. Saturday __________ Monday
5. Thursday __________ Saturday
6. Sunday __________ Tuesday

10

STUDENT BOOK PAGES **87–96**

B WHAT ARE THEY SAYING?

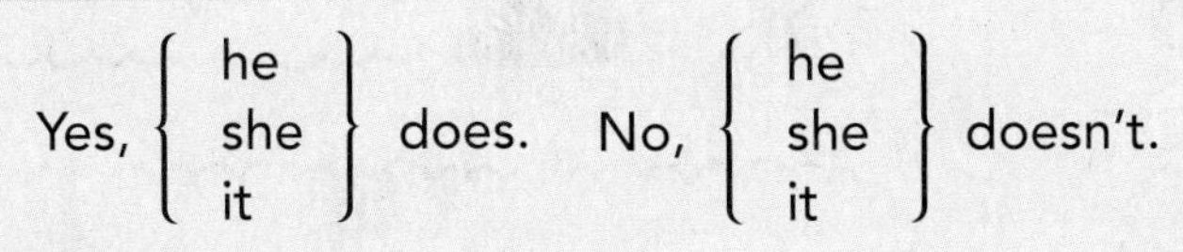

what kind of
when

1. ___Does___ your husband cook breakfast every day?
   Yes, ___he does___.

2. __________ your daughter study English in school?
   Yes, __________.

3. __________ your son drive a car?
   No, __________.

4. __________ food does he cook?
   He cooks Italian food.

5. __________ that dog live in this neighborhood?
   No, it __________.

6. __________ your grandfather shop at the grocery store in his neighborhood?
   Yes, __________.

7. __________ your sister work at the bank?
   No, __________.

8. __________ does Robert visit his friends?
   He visits his friends on Sunday.

C WHAT ARE THEY SAYING?

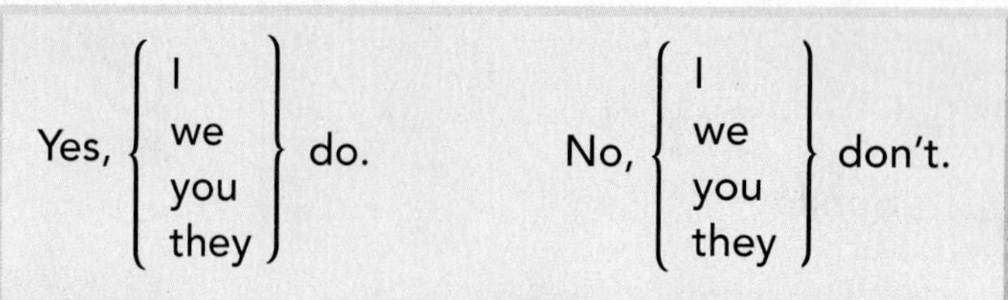

Yes, { I / we / you / they } do.
No, { I / we / you / they } don't.

1. 

2. 

3. 

4. 

5. 

6. 

D LISTENING

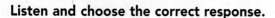

Listen and choose the correct response.

1. a. Chinese music.
   (b.) French food.
   c. Every day.

2. a. Yes, he does.
   b. No, we don't.
   c. Yes, they do.

3. a. No, he doesn't.
   b. Because he likes the food.
   c. On Wednesday.

4. a. On Sunday.
   b. Yes, she does.
   c. In her house.

5. a. I go every day.
   b. I don't go there.
   c. Yes, I do.

6. a. In New York.
   b. On Thursday.
   c. They don't go there.

7. a. Because it's open.
   b. They play.
   c. He rides his bicycle.

8. a. No, they don't.
   b. In the city.
   c. Yes, she does.

9. a. Because it's near their house.
   b. On Central Avenue.
   c. Yes, they do.

E YES AND NO

1. My husband cooks Italian food. He __doesn't__ __cook__ Thai food.
2. Linda drives a taxi. She ________ ________ a bus.
3. Our children play the piano. They ________ ________ the guitar.
4. I work on Saturday. I ________ ________ on Sunday.
5. Tom lives in an apartment. He ________ ________ in a house.
6. My wife and I exercise in the park. We ________ ________ in a health club.
7. Every Saturday Mrs. Roberts ________ to the library. She doesn't go to the mall.
8. I ________ in large supermarkets. I don't shop in small grocery stores.
9. My mother ________ stockings. She doesn't wear socks.
10. Omar ________ Arabic. He doesn't speak Spanish.
11. Harry sings in the shower. He ________ ________ in the jacuzzi.

F WHAT'S THE WORD?

do	does

1. Where __do__ they live?
2. When ________ your daughter do her homework?
3. What kind of books ________ you read?
4. Why ________ he call you every day?
5. What languages ________ they speak?
6. Where ________ your husband work?
7. ________ you visit your friends every week?
8. ________ he go to Stanley's Restaurant?
9. When ________ you go to the supermarket?
10. ________ your children wash the dishes?
11. What kind of music ________ she listen to?
12. What ________ he sell?
13. Why ________ they cry at weddings?

G WRITE ABOUT YOURSELF

1. I like .... I don't like ....
2. I play .... I don't play ....
3. I speak .... I don't speak ....
4. I eat .... I don't eat ....
5. I cook .... I don't cook ....

H YES OR NO?

1. Does Kathy take karate lessons?

   Yes, she does.

2. Do Jim and Tom play tennis on Sunday?

   No, they don't. They play volleyball.

3. Do you and Harry go dancing on Friday?

   ____

4. Does Miguel play in the orchestra?

   ____

5. Do you see a movie every weekend?

   ____

6. Do Mr. and Mrs. Kim go to a health club?

   ____

7. Does Richard jog in the park?

   ____

8. Do you and your wife watch TV every day?

   ____

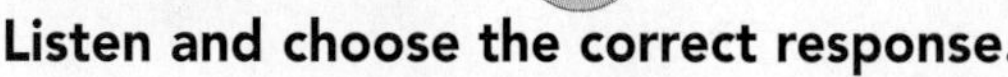

I LISTENING

Listen and choose the correct response.

1. a. Yes, they do.
   (b.) Yes, I do.
2. a. Yes, he does.
   b. Yes, I do.
3. a. No, he doesn't.
   b. No, they don't.
4. a. No, she doesn't.
   b. No, I don't.
5. a. Yes, we do.
   b. Yes, he does.
6. a. Yes, we do.
   b. No, they don't.
7. a. No, I don't.
   b. Yes, he does.
8. a. Yes, they do.
   b. Yes, he does.
9. a. No, we don't.
   b. No, they don't.

J GrammarRap: *They Do, They Don't* 

Listen. Then clap and practice.

Does he   Yes he   No he

A. Does he eat French bread?
B. Yes, he does.
A. Does she like Swiss cheese?
B. Yes, she does.

A. Do they cook Greek food?
B. Yes, they do.
A. Do they speak Chinese?
B. Yes, they do.

All. He eats French bread.
She likes Swiss cheese.
They cook Greek food.
And they speak Chinese.

A. Does he read the paper?
B. No, he doesn't.
A. Does she watch TV?
B. No, she doesn't.

A. Do they go to movies?
B. No, they don't.
A. Do they drink iced tea?
B. No, they don't.

All. He doesn't read the paper.
She doesn't watch TV.
They don't go to movies.
And they don't drink tea.

K A LETTER TO A PEN PAL

Read and practice.

Wednesday

Dear Peter,

My family and I live in San Juan. We speak Spanish. My mother is a music teacher. She plays the violin and the piano. My father works in an office.

My brother Ramon and I go to school every day. We study history, English, Spanish, science, and mathematics. My favorite school subject is science. I don't like history, but I like mathematics.

Do you like sports? Every day at school I play soccer. On Saturday I swim. What sports do you play? What kind of music do you like? I like rock music and country music very much, but I don't like jazz. What kind of movies do you like? I like adventure movies and comedies. I think science fiction movies are terrible.

Tell me about your family and your school.

Your friend,
Maria

L YOUR LETTER TO A PEN PAL

history
English
mathematics
science
music

baseball
football
hockey
golf
tennis
soccer

cartoons
dramas
comedies
westerns
adventure movies
science fiction movies

classical music
jazz
popular music
rock music
country music

Dear ....,

My family and I live in .... We speak .... At school, I study ...., ..., and .... My favorite subject is .... I don't like ....

What sports do you play? I play .... and .... I think .... is wonderful. I don't like ....

What kind of movies do you like? I like .... and ....

My favorite kind of music is ...., and I like .... I don't listen to ....

Tell me about your school and your city.

Your friend,

....

✓ CHECK-UP TEST: Chapters 9–10

A. Circle the correct answers.

Ex. We (live) / lives in Tokyo.

1. Tom play / plays in the park.

2. My wife and I shop / shops on Monday.

3. She don't / doesn't work on Saturday.

4. Where do / does your cousins live?

5. We stays / stay home every Sunday.

6. What activities do / does she do?

B. Fill in the blanks.

Ex. What is your address?

1. ________ does he live?
2. ________ kind of food do you like?
3. ________ Patty baby-sit for her neighbors?
4. ________ do you eat at that restaurant?
   Because we like the food.
5. ________ does Julie go to a health club?
   On Monday.
6. ________ does your family do on Sunday?

C. Fill in the blanks.

Mrs. Davis ________[1] in Dallas. She's a very active person. She ________[2] exercises every day. On Monday she ________[3] her apartment, on Wednesday she ________[4] tennis, on Friday she ________[5] a karate lesson, on Saturday she ________[6] her bicycle in the park, and on Sunday she ________[7] to a museum and ________[8] lunch in a restaurant.

D. Listen and choose the correct response.

Ex. a. We go to school.
(b.) They work in an office.
c. They're shy.

1. a. Yes, we do.
   b. We like dramas.
   c. On Thursday.

2. a. In a restaurant.
   b. Because we like it.
   c. Every day.

3. a. Yes, they do.
   b. Yes, he does.
   c. In Puerto Rico.

4. a. Short stories.
   b. News programs.
   c. I like golf.

5. a. Yes, they do.
   b. Because it's convenient.
   c. On Center Street.

A LANGUAGE

Read the article on student book page 97 and answer the questions.

SIDE by SIDE Gazette

STUDENT BOOK PAGES **97–98**

1. There are ______ languages in the world.
   a. five hundred
   b. millions of
   c. twenty thousand
   d. more than twenty thousand

2. ______ is a very rare language.
   a. Chinese
   b. Spanish
   c. Bahinemo
   d. Arabic

3. The word *ketchup* is from ______.
   a. Chinese
   b. French
   c. Spanish
   d. Arabic

4. The word *cyberspace* comes from ______.
   a. French
   b. Spanish
   c. Arabic
   d. technology

5. The word ______ is from Arabic.
   a. *rodeo*
   b. *sofa*
   c. *potato*
   d. *cafe*

6. According to this article, Portuguese is a ______ language.
   a. difficult
   b. common
   c. rare
   d. new

7. Bahinemo is a language from ______.
   a. China
   b. the United States
   c. Japan
   d. Papua, New Guinea

8. *Borrow* in paragraph 2 means ______.
   a. speak
   b. study
   c. take
   d. give

9. *Recent* in paragraph 2 means ______.
   a. new
   b. difficult
   c. interesting
   d. common

10. ______ is a recent word.
    a. *Ketchup*
    b. *Website*
    c. *Potato*
    d. *Rodeo*

B BUILD YOUR VOCABULARY!

Choose the correct word.

1. I comb my (hair teeth).
2. She (goes gets) up, and then she (goes gets) dressed.
3. I sit and relax when I take a (shower bath).
4. He (eats brushes his teeth) after breakfast, lunch, and dinner.
5. She (takes cleans) a shower every morning.
6. I don't get (dressed up) on Sunday morning. I eat breakfast in my pajamas.
7. Rosa goes to (work bed) at 12:00 every night and gets up at 7:00.
8. Martin cooks in a restaurant on weekends. He goes to (work school) every Saturday and Sunday.
9. Tina doesn't eat breakfast because she (gets up goes to bed) late.

C FACT FILE

Look at the Fact File on student book page 97 and answer the questions.

1. Three hundred twenty-two million people speak ______.
   a. Russian
   b. Arabic
   c. Spanish
   d. English

2. One hundred eighty-two million people speak ______.
   a. Japanese
   b. Bengali
   c. Hindi
   d. Portuguese

3. There are ______ Arabic speakers.
   a. three hundred thirty-two million
   b. two hundred sixty-eight million
   c. one hundred seventy million
   d. eight hundred eighty-five million

4. More than three hundred million people speak ______.
   a. Russian
   b. Bengali
   c. Spanish
   d. Arabic

5. There are ______ Japanese speakers.
   a. one hundred twenty-five million
   b. one hundred eighty-nine million
   c. ninety-eight million
   d. one hundred eighty-nine million

6. There are the same number of Portuguese and ______ speakers.
   a. German
   b. Bengali
   c. Hindi
   d. Russian

7. More than eight hundred million people speak ______.
   a. English
   b. Chinese
   c. Hindi and Portuguese
   d. Arabic and Bengali

8. Spanish and ______ are common languages in South America.
   a. Portuguese
   b. Japanese
   c. Bengali
   d. Arabic

D "CAN-DO" REVIEW

Match the "can do" statement and the correct sentence.

____ **1.** I can ask a person's name.	**a.**	I speak Spanish.
____ **2.** I can tell where I live.	**b.**	I drive a bus.
____ **3.** I can tell what language I speak.	**c.**	My sister is an outgoing person.
____ **4.** I can tell about my nationality.	**d.**	I like Greek food.
____ **5.** I can tell about my work.	**e.**	I live in Seoul.
____ **6.** I can ask about a person's work.	**f.**	I don't like American food.
____ **7.** I can talk about likes.	**g.**	I'm Mexican.
____ **8.** I can talk about dislikes.	**h.**	What kind of music do you like?
____ **9.** I can describe people.	**i.**	What do you do?
____ **10.** I can ask questions to make small talk.	**j.**	What's your name?

A WHAT ARE THEY SAYING?

STUDENT BOOK
PAGES **99–106**

me	us
him	you
her	them
it	

1. Do you like me?
   Of course I like _you_.

2. Do you like your neighbors?
   Of course I like ________.

3. Do you like Helen?
   Of course I like ________.

4. Do you like George?
   Of course I like ________.

5. Do you like videos?
   Of course I like ________.

6. Do you like English?
   Of course I like ________.

7. Do your friends like you?
   Of course they like ________.

8. Do you like your new apartment?
   Of course I like ________.

9. Does your dog like you?
   Of course he likes ________.

B WHAT'S THE WORD?

it	her	him	them

1. She washes ___it___ every morning.

2. I think about ________ all the time.

3. We visit ________ every weekend.

4. I talk to ________ every night.

5. He uses ________ every day.

6. We feed ________ every afternoon.

C LISTENING 

Listen and put a check (✓) under the correct picture.

1. ______ ___✓___

2. ______ ______

3. ______ ______

4. ______ ______

5. ______ ______

6. ______ ______

D WRITE ABOUT YOURSELF

1. I .... every day.
2. I .... every week.
3. I .... every month.
4. I .... every year.
5. I .... every weekend.
6. I .... every Sunday.
7. I .... every morning.
8. I .... all the time.

E WRITE IT AND SAY IT

Write the correct form of the word in parentheses and then say the sentence.

1. Carol sometimes (eat) ___eats___ Thai food.
2. My neighbor's dog always (bark) ________ in the afternoon.
3. My son never (clean) ________ his bedroom.
4. Ray always (wash) ________ his car on the weekend.
5. My brother sometimes (jog) ________ at night.
6. Amy usually (read) ________ poetry.
7. My mother rarely (shop) ________ at the grocery store around the corner.
8. Dan sometimes (watch) ________ videos on Saturday.
9. Omar usually (speak) ________ English at work.
10. Patty usually (play) ________ tennis in the park on Saturday.

F MATCHING

c	1. Walter always washes his car on Sunday.	a.	She usually watches dramas.
____	2. Jonathan never cooks dinner.	b.	He rarely jogs at night.
____	3. Carla rarely watches comedies.	c.	He never washes it during the week.
____	4. My grandmother rarely speaks English.	d.	She usually studies in the library.
____	5. Richard usually jogs in the morning.	e.	He always eats in a restaurant.
____	6. Larry never writes letters.	f.	He always writes e-mail messages.
____	7. Nancy rarely studies at home.	g.	She usually speaks Spanish.
____	8. Jane always fixes her computer.	h.	She never calls a repairperson.

G LISTENING 

Listen and choose the correct answer.

1. a. He usually washes it.
   (b.) He never washes it.
2. a. My husband sometimes cooks.
   b. My husband never cooks.
3. a. My neighbors are quiet.
   b. My neighbors are noisy.
4. a. They usually speak Spanish.
   b. They usually speak English.
5. a. Jane is shy.
   b. Jane is outgoing.
6. a. I usually study at home.
   b. I usually study in the library.

H WRITE ABOUT YOURSELF

always	usually	sometimes	rarely	never

1. I .... wear glasses.
2. I .... eat Italian food.
3. I .... listen to country music.
4. I .... go to English class.
5. I .... watch videos.
6. I .... read poetry.
7. I .... fix my car.
8. I .... visit my grandparents.
9. I .... watch game shows on TV.
10. I .... use a cell phone.
11. I .... clean my apartment.
12. I always ....
13. I usually ....
14. I sometimes ....
15. I rarely ....
16. I never ....

I GRAMMARRAP: *I Always Get to Work on Time*

Listen. Then clap and practice.

A. I always get to work on time.
I'm usually here by eight.
I sometimes get here early.
I never get here late.
No, I never get here late.

B. He always gets to work on time.
He's usually here by eight.
He sometimes gets here early.
He rarely gets here late.

A. No! I NEVER get here late.

B. Right! He never gets here late.

J WHAT'S THE WORD?

have has

1. Do you ___have___ a bicycle?
2. My daughter __________ curly hair.
3. My parents __________ an old car.
4. Does your son __________ blond hair?
5. Our building __________ a satellite dish.
6. Do you __________ large sunglasses?
7. My sister __________ green eyes.
8. We __________ two dogs and a cat.

K WHAT ARE THEY SAYING?

have has do does don't doesn't

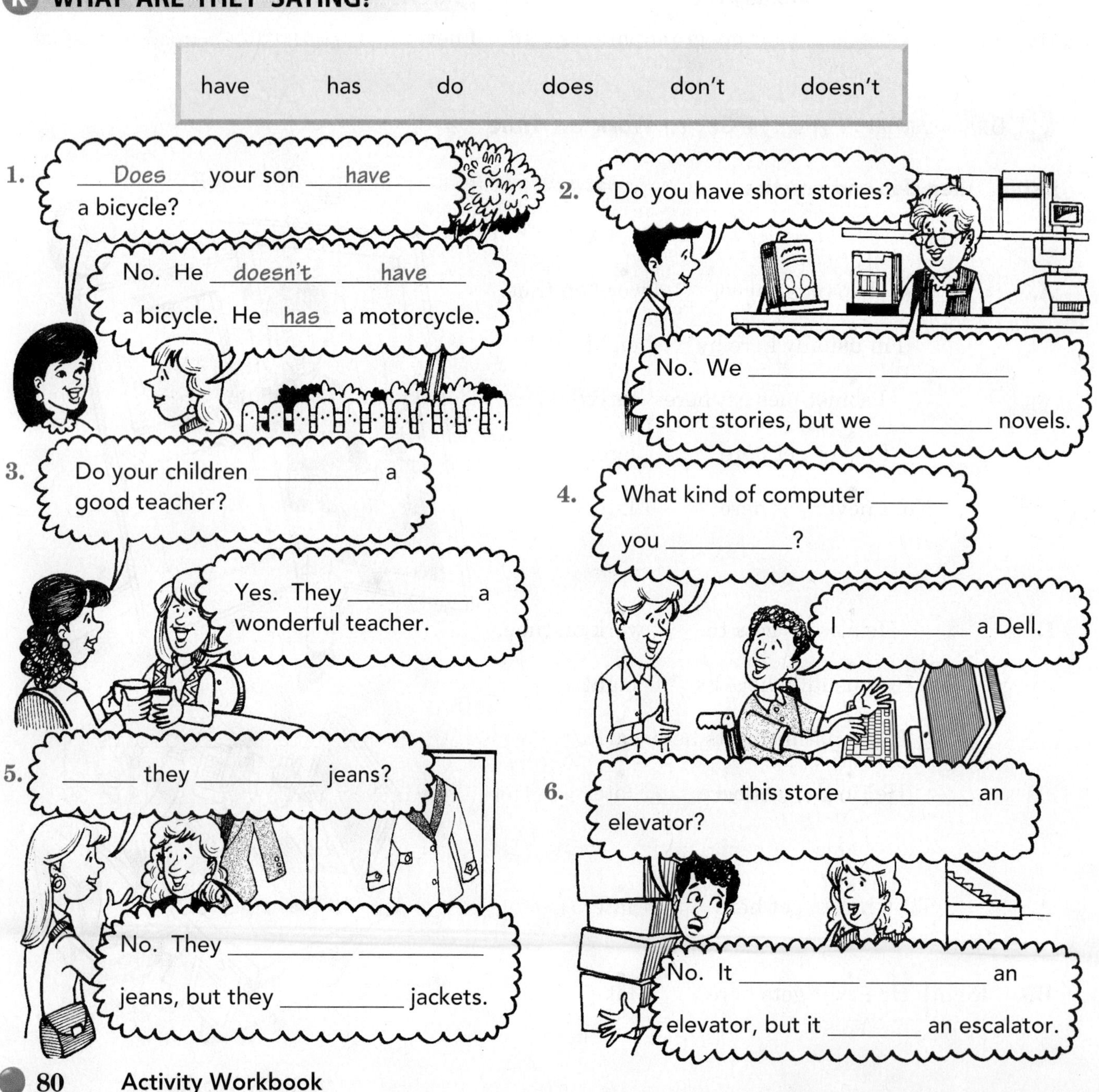

1.
___Does___ your son ___have___ a bicycle?
No. He ___doesn't___ ___have___ a bicycle. He ___has___ a motorcycle.
2.
Do you have short stories?
No. We __________ __________ short stories, but we __________ novels.
3.
Do your children __________ a good teacher?
Yes. They __________ a wonderful teacher.
4.
What kind of computer ______ you __________?
I __________ a Dell.
5.
______ they __________ jeans?
No. They __________ __________ jeans, but they __________ jackets.
6.
__________ this store __________ an elevator?
No. It __________ __________ an elevator, but it ________ an escalator.

L WHAT'S THE WORD?

1. Tina doesn't have short hair. She has (long / curly) hair.

2. I don't have straight hair. I have (thin / curly) hair.

3. My brother isn't tall. He's (heavy / short).

4. Albert isn't married. He's (curly / single).

5. Your baby boy has beautiful blond (eyes / hair).

6. His eyes aren't blue. They're (brown / straight).

7. We don't live in the city. We live in the (house / suburbs).

M TWO BROTHERS

My brother and I are very different. I'm tall, and he's short 1. I ________ 2 brown eyes, and he ________ 3 blue eyes. We both ________ 4 brown hair, but I have long, straight hair, and he has ________ 5, ________ 6 hair. I'm short and heavy. And he's ________ 7 and ________ 8. I'm a chef, and ________ 9 a doctor. I live in New York. He ________ 10 in San Diego. I have a small apartment in the city. He ________ 11 a large house ________ 12 the suburbs. I play tennis. He ________ 13 golf. I play the guitar. He doesn't ________ 14 a musical instrument. On the weekend, I usually ________ 15 to parties. He doesn't ________ 16 to parties. He ________ 17 TV and ________ 18 the newspaper.

N LISTENING

Listen and choose the correct response.

1. a. No. I have short hair.
   (b.) No. I have straight hair.
2. a. No. I'm single.
   b. No. I'm tall and thin.
3. a. No. He has black eyes.
   b. No. He has brown eyes.
4. a. No. This is my mother.
   b. No. I have a sister.
5. a. Yes. I go to parties.
   b. Yes. I stay home.
6. a. Yes. He's thin.
   b. No. He's thin.
7. a. No. I live in an apartment.
   b. No. I live in the suburbs.
8. a. No. I have long hair.
   b. No. I have curly hair.

O WHAT'S THE WORD?

Circle the correct word.

1. He watches TV [at / with / (in)] the evening.
2. The health club is [in / on / between] Main Street.
3. I'm playing a game [on / to / in] my computer.
4. Ann is sleeping [on / in / across] the yard.
5. He always talks [about / to / with] the weather.
6. I'm looking [from / for / to] a striped shirt.
7. Do you live [in / on / at] the suburbs?
8. Do your children go [to / at / in] school every day?
9. Tim is swimming [with / on / at] the beach.
10. My son is wearing a pair [from / for / of] new jeans.
11. Do you go [in / to / at] work [at / in / on] Saturday?
12. I listen [to / at / on] the radio in the morning.

A WHAT'S THE WORD?

angry	embarrassed	hot	nervous	scared	thirsty
cold	happy	hungry	sad	sick	tired

1. Howard is crying. He's ___sad___.

2. Helen is yawning. She's ______________.

3. Sam is perspiring. He's ______________.

4. Frank is shouting. He's ______________.

5. Mrs. Allen is going to the hospital.

   She's ______________.

6. Peter is looking at his paper and smiling.

   He's ______________.

7. Ben's cat is eating. It's ______________.

8. Irene is shivering. She's ______________.

9. Louise is biting her nails.

   She's ______________.

10. Jason is covering his eyes.

    He's ______________.

11. Pam is drinking milk.

    She's ______________.

12. Bobby is blushing.

    He's ______________.

B TELL ME WHY

1. A. Why are they yawning?

   B. They're yawning because they're tired.

   They always yawn when they're tired.

2. A. Why is she crying?

   B. ______________________________ sad.

   She always ______________________.

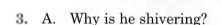

3. A. Why is he shivering?

   B. ______________________________ cold.

   He always ______________________.

4. A. Why are you perspiring?

   B. ______________________________ hot.

   I always ______________________.

5. A. Why is she smiling?

   B. ______________________________ happy.

   She always ______________________.

6. A. Why are they eating?

   B. ______________________________ hungry.

   They always ______________________.

7. A. Why are you shouting?

   B. ______________________________ angry.

   We always ______________________.

8. A. Why is he covering his eyes?

   B. ______________________________ scared.

   He always ______________________.

C GrammarRap: *I Smile When I'm Happy* 

Listen. Then clap and practice.

A. I smile when I'm happy.
I frown when I'm sad.
I blush when I'm embarrassed.
And I shout when I'm mad.

B. Are you smiling?
A. Yes. I'm happy.
B. Are you frowning?
A. Yes. I'm sad.
B. Are you blushing?
A. I'm embarrassed.
B. Are you shouting?
A. Yes. I'm mad.

D GrammarRap: *Why Are You Doing That?* 

Listen. Then clap and practice.

A. What's Fran doing?
B. She's working late.
A. Working late?
Why's she doing that?
B. It's Monday.
She always works late on Monday.

A. What are you doing?
B. We're playing cards.
A. Playing cards?
Why are you doing that?
B. It's Tuesday.
We always play cards on Tuesday.

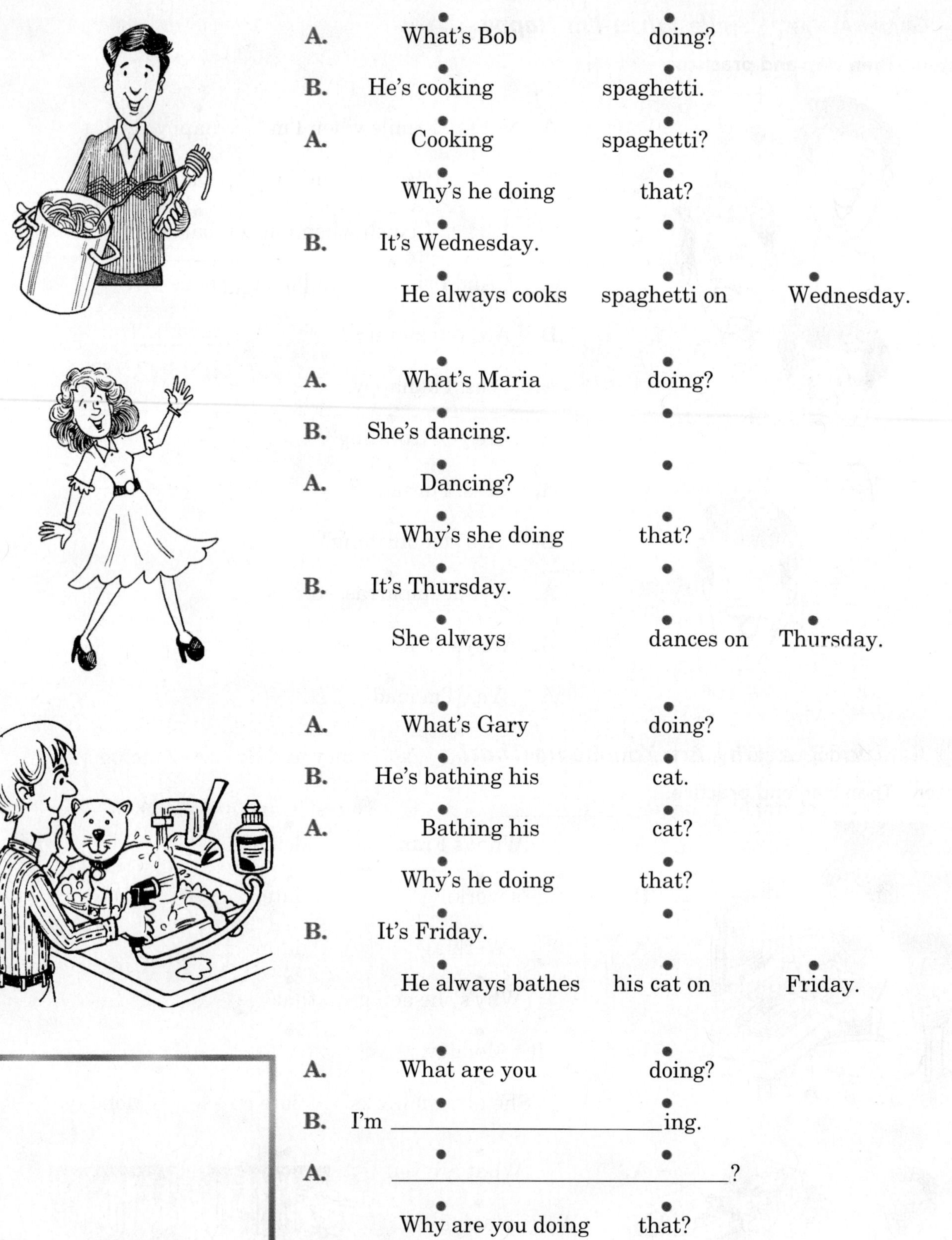

A. What's Bob doing?
B. He's cooking spaghetti.
A. Cooking spaghetti?
Why's he doing that?
B. It's Wednesday.
He always cooks spaghetti on Wednesday.

A. What's Maria doing?
B. She's dancing.
A. Dancing?
Why's she doing that?
B. It's Thursday.
She always dances on Thursday.

A. What's Gary doing?
B. He's bathing his cat.
A. Bathing his cat?
Why's he doing that?
B. It's Friday.
He always bathes his cat on Friday.

A. What are you doing?
B. I'm ______________________ing.
A. ______________________?
Why are you doing that?
B. It's Saturday.
I always ____________________ on Saturday.

E THAT'S STRANGE!

1. A. My sister is cooking dinner today.
   B. That's strange! She never ___cooks___ dinner.

2. A. Our children are studying with a flashlight.
   B. That's strange! They never __________ with a flashlight.

3. A. Victor is walking to work today.
   B. That's strange! He never __________ to work.

4. A. Ann is brushing her teeth in the kitchen.
   B. That's strange! She never __________ her teeth in the kitchen.

5. A. The dog is eating in the dining room today.
   B. That's strange! It never __________ in the dining room.

6. A. Nancy and Bob are dancing in the office.
   B. That's strange! They never __________ in the office.

7. A. Ruth __________________ the carpet today.
   B. That's strange! She never sweeps the carpet.

8. A. My parents __________________ poetry today.
   B. That's strange! They never read poetry.

9. A. ______________ a typewriter today.
   B. That's strange! You never use a typewriter.

10. A. My cousins __________________ in the yard.
    B. That's strange! They never sleep in the yard.

F WHAT'S THE QUESTION?

Choose the correct question word. Then write the question.

What	When	Where	Why	What kind of	How many

1. I'm blushing because I'm embarrassed. _Why are you blushing?_
2. They play tennis in the park. ______________
3. She reads her e-mail at night. ______________
4. I like Brazilian food. ______________
5. We have ten cats. ______________
6. He's using his cell phone. ______________

What	How often	Where	Why	What kind of	How many

7. He watches game shows. ______________
8. We call our grandchildren every week. ______________
9. They play golf every weekend. ______________
10. I'm smiling because I'm happy. ______________
11. She's eating in the cafeteria today. ______________
12. I'm wearing two sweaters. ______________

G WHICH ONE DOESN'T BELONG?

1.	her	me	them	(we)
2.	noisy	usually	sometimes	rarely
3.	does	doesn't	has	don't
4.	angry	yoga	nervous	happy
5.	Wednesday	Why	What	When
6.	smiling	shivering	crying	outgoing
7.	clean	sweep	shy	wash
8.	year	evening	night	afternoon

H LISTENING 

As you listen to each story, read the sentences and check *yes* or *no*.

Jennifer and Jason

1. yes ☐ no ☑ Jennifer and Jason are visiting their father.
2. yes ☐ no ☐ Jennifer and Jason are happy.
3. yes ☐ no ☐ Their grandfather isn't taking them to the park.

Our Boss

4. yes ☐ no ☐ Our boss usually smiles at the office.
5. yes ☐ no ☐ He's happy today.
6. yes ☐ no ☐ Everyone is thinking about the weekend.

On Vacation

7. yes ☐ no ☐ I like vacations.
8. yes ☐ no ☐ When the weather is nice, I watch videos.
9. yes ☐ no ☐ I'm swimming at the beach today because it's cold.

Timmy and His Brother

10. yes ☐ no ☐ Timmy is covering his eyes because he's sad.
11. yes ☐ no ☐ Timmy doesn't like science fiction movies.
12. yes ☐ no ☐ Timmy's brother is scared.

I LOUD AND CLEAR 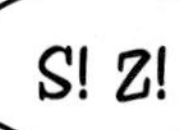

sorry hospital sick sister Sally

1. Sally is sorry her sister is sick in the hospital.

scientist speaking What's experiments

2. ______ the ______ doing? He's ______ about his new ______.

always	cousin	Athens	busy	is

3. My ________ in ________ ____ ________ very ________.

doesn't	Sally's	clothes	husband	closet

4. ________ ________ ________ have any clean ________ in his ________.

Steven	it's	sweeping	is	because

5. ________ ____ ________ the floor ________ ____ dirty.

Sunday	Mrs.	newspaper	Garcia	reads

6. ________ ________ ________ the ________ every ________.

zoo	students	sometimes	bus	school

7. The ________ in our ________ ________ go to the ____ on the ____.

plays	soccer	friends	Tuesday	son

8. My ____ Sam ________ ________ with his ________ every ________.

✓ CHECK-UP TEST: Chapters 11–12

A. Fill in the blanks.

me him her it us you them

Ex. Do you like this book?
Of course I like ___it___.

1. Do you look like your father?
   Yes. I look like ________.
2. When my cats are hungry, I always feed ________.
3. Sally rarely plays with her sister, but she's playing with ________ today.
4. I say "hello" to my boss every day, and he says "hello" to ________.
5. We're going to the park. Do you want to go with ______?

B. Fill in the blanks.

Ex. Betty never talks to her landlord, but she's ___talking___ to him today.

1. We never feed the birds, but we're ____________ them today.
2. Harriet never __________ to parties, but she's going to a party today.
3. My children never bake, but they're __________ today.
4. Tim never __________ his TV, but he's fixing it today.
5. Amy rarely __________ her kitchen windows, but she's washing them today.

C. Fill in the blanks.

do does is are

Ex. a. What ___do___ you usually do on the weekend?
b. What ___is___ Tina doing today?

1. Why ______ the baby crying?
2. When ______ David and Pam go to the supermarket?
3. ________ Bob usually dance?
4. Do they work here? Yes, they ______.
5. ________ your parents cooking lunch?

D. Write the question.

Ex. I'm shivering <u>because I'm cold</u>. (Why?)
___Why are you shivering?___

1. They work <u>in a laboratory</u> every day. (Where?)
   ____
2. We get together <u>on Saturday</u>. (When?)
   ____
3. He's crying <u>because he's sad</u>. (Why?)
   ____
4. She has <u>three</u> children. (How many?)
   ____
5. I'm drinking <u>milk</u>. (What?)
   ____

E. Listen and choose the correct response.

Ex. (a.) They're playing soccer.
b. They play tennis.

1. a. They're delivering mail.
   b. They deliver mail.
2. a. We're going to the zoo.
   b. We go to the park.
3. a. I'm covering my eyes.
   b. I cover my eyes.
4. a. No, I don't.
   b. No, I'm not.
5. a. I'm studying in the library.
   b. I study in the library.

A TRAFFIC: A Global Problem

SIDE by SIDE Gazette

STUDENT BOOK PAGES 115–116

Read the article on student book page 115 and answer the questions.

1. Rush hour is the time when ______.
   a. people are busy at work
   b. people are busy at home
   c. people go to work
   d. the roads are empty

2. Some ______ have carpool lanes.
   a. bus systems
   b. highways
   c. subway systems
   d. license plates

3. Carpool lanes are for ______.
   a. cars with two or more people
   b. cars with special license plates
   c. all cars during rush hour
   d. cars on two or three days of the week

4. *Cities are expanding their bus and subway systems* means ______.
   a. cities are painting them
   b. cities are cleaning them
   c. cities are fixing them
   d. there are more and more buses and subways in these cities

5. Many cities are trying to reduce ______.
   a. the traffic on their roads
   b. their highways
   c. their carpool lanes
   d. their bus and subway systems

6. Traffic is a big problem in cities around the world because many people ______.
   a. take buses to work
   b. drive to work
   c. take trains to work
   d. take subways to work

7. In Athens people with license plate numbers ending in 4 ______.
   a. drive their cars four days a week
   b. drive their cars every day of the week
   c. drive their cars in special lanes
   d. don't drive their cars every day of the week

8. *Traffic is a global problem* means ______.
   a. traffic is a problem in Athens
   b. traffic is a difficult problem
   c. traffic is a problem around the world
   d. traffic is a problem today

B BUILD YOUR VOCABULARY!

Choose the correct word.

1. My office is around the corner from my house so I (walk take the bus) to work.
2. I ride a (motorcycle bicycle) to work because it's a good way to exercise.
3. I live in the suburbs and take the (train subway) to work. I sit at a window and I look at the people and houses outside.
4. I (ride a motor scooter drive) to work. It's a good way to get there except when it rains.
5. I take the (subway bus) to work. When there's a lot of traffic it takes thirty minutes.
6. I (ride a motorcycle drive) to work. It's noisy, but it's fun in good weather.
7. Sometimes when I'm very late for work I (ride a bicycle take a taxi).
8. I (drive walk) to work on a very busy highway.
9. I (ride a motor scooter take the subway) to work. Sometimes there are a lot of people, and there isn't a place to sit.

C FACT FILE

Look at the Fact File on student book page 116 and answer the questions.

1. More than seven hundred million people ride the subway in São Paulo in a ______.
   a. month
   b. year
   c. week
   d. day

2. Seven hundred seventy-nine million people ride the subway in ______ in a year.
   a. Hong Kong
   b. Tokyo
   c. São Paulo
   d. London

3. ______ people ride the subway in Moscow in a year.
   a. 3,160
   b. 31,600
   c. 3,160,000
   d. 3,160,000,000

4. The largest subway systems in the world have _____ riders.
   a. hundreds of
   b. thousands of
   c. a million
   d. millions of

5. The subway system in Seoul has 1,390,000,000 riders, but the subway system in ______ has even more riders.
   a. London
   b. Mexico City
   c. Hong Kong
   d. Paris

6. The subway system in ______ has 1,000,000,000 riders.
   a. Tokyo
   b. New York
   c. Osaka
   d. Paris

7. ______ people ride the subway in Paris in a year.
   a. 1,120,000,000
   b. 1,420,000,000
   c. 2,740,000,000
   d. 1,130,000,000

8. Two of the world's largest subway systems are in ______.
   a. Russia
   b. England
   c. Japan
   d. Mexico

D "CAN-DO" REVIEW

Match the "can do" statement and the correct sentence.

____ 1.	I can talk about common activities.	a.	Tell me about your children.
____ 2.	I can describe people.	b.	I'm a scientist.
____ 3.	I can give my occupation.	c.	Oh, really? That's interesting.
____ 4.	I can give my marital status.	d.	What are you doing?
____ 5.	I can ask for information.	e.	I'm happy.
____ 6.	I can react to information.	f.	My computer is broken.
____ 7.	I can describe my emotions.	g.	I usually watch the news after dinner.
____ 8.	I can ask about a person's activity.	h.	I'm single.
____ 9.	I can describe a repair problem.	i.	When I'm embarrassed, I blush.
____ 10.	I can describe how I react to things.	j.	My sister has short, curly hair.

A CAN OR CAN'T?

cook	drive	play	skate	speak
dance	paint	sing	ski	use

1. Billy __can't__ __ski__.

   He __can__ __skate__.

2. Sally ________ ________.

   She ________ ________.

3. Edward ________ ________ pictures.

   He ________ ________ houses.

4. Carla ________ ________ Arabic.

   She ________ ________ Italian.

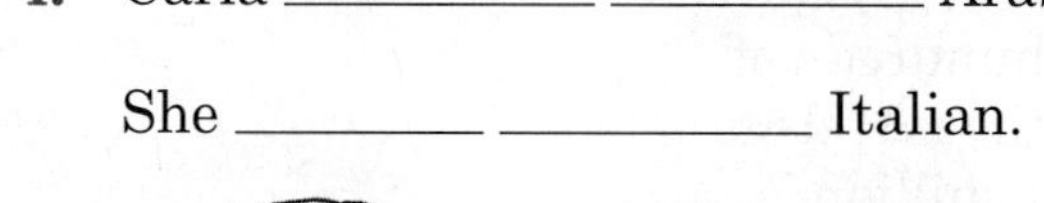

5. We ________ ________ Greek food.

   We ________ ________ Japanese food.

6. I ________ ________ a cash register.

   I ________ ________ a calculator.

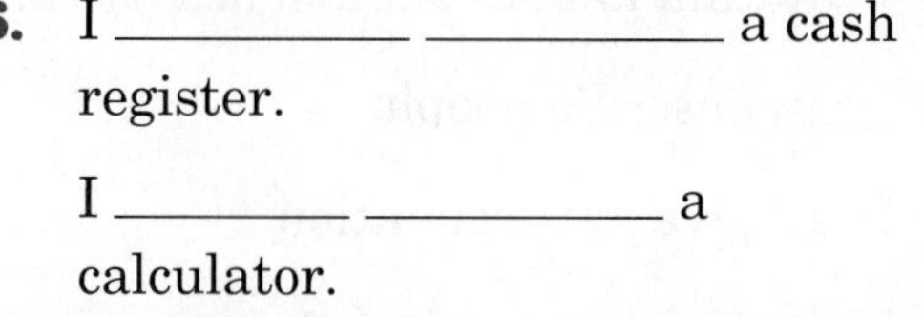

7. They ________ ________ tennis.

   They ________ ________ baseball.

8. Harold ________ ________ a taxi.

   He ________ ________ a bus.

B WHAT CAN YOU DO?

Check the things you can do. Then ask other students.

Can you . . .?	*You*		*Student 1*		*Student 2*	
1. cook	❑ yes	❑ no	❑ yes	❑ no	❑ yes	❑ no
2. swim	❑ yes	❑ no	❑ yes	❑ no	❑ yes	❑ no
3. ski	❑ yes	❑ no	❑ yes	❑ no	❑ yes	❑ no
4. skate	❑ yes	❑ no	❑ yes	❑ no	❑ yes	❑ no
5. paint	❑ yes	❑ no	❑ yes	❑ no	❑ yes	❑ no
6. drive	❑ yes	❑ no	❑ yes	❑ no	❑ yes	❑ no
7. play tennis	❑ yes	❑ no	❑ yes	❑ no	❑ yes	❑ no
8. speak Chinese	❑ yes	❑ no	❑ yes	❑ no	❑ yes	❑ no
9. use a cash register	❑ yes	❑ no	❑ yes	❑ no	❑ yes	❑ no

C WHAT'S THE QUESTION?

1. ______Can he cook______?
Yes, he can.

2. ______________________?
No, she can't.

3. ______________________?
Yes, they can.

4. ______________________?
Yes, I can.

5. ______________________?
No, he can't.

6. ______________________?
No, we can't.

D LISTENING 

Listen and circle the word you hear.

1.	(can)	can't	4.	can	can't	7.	can	can't	10.	can	can't
2.	can	can't	5.	can	can't	8.	can	can't	11.	can	can't
3.	can	can't	6.	can	can't	9.	can	can't	12.	can	can't

E PUZZLE

actor actress baker chef dancer mechanic secretary singer teacher truck driver

Across

4. She fixes cars every day.
6. He teaches in a school.
7. She acts in the movies.
9. He dances every day.
10. He acts on TV.

Down

1. She drives a truck.
2. He types every day.
3. He cooks in a restaurant.
5. He bakes pies and cakes.
8. She sings on TV.

F *CAN* OR *CAN'T*?

1. My brother is a chef in a bakery. He ___can___ bake pies and cakes.
2. They ___can't___ sing. They aren't very good singers.
3. __________ Jane drive a truck? Of course she __________.
   She's a truck driver.
4. The chef in that restaurant __________ cook!
   The food is terrible!
5. Of course I __________ fix cars. I'm a mechanic.
6. That actor is terrible! He __________ act!
7. __________ they dance? Of course they __________.
   They're dancers on TV.
8. I'm a very good cashier. I __________ use a cash register.
9. My new secretary isn't very good. He __________ type, and he __________ speak on the telephone.
10. They're very athletic. They __________ skate, they __________ ski, and they __________ play soccer.
11. My friend George can only speak English. He __________ speak Spanish, and he __________ speak French.

G GrammarRap: *Of Course They Can!*

Listen. Then clap and practice.

> She can speak.
> He can speak.
> We can speak.
> They can speak.

A. Can Anne speak French?
B. Of course she can.
She can speak French very well.

A. Can the Browns play tennis?
B. Of course they can.
They can play tennis very well.

A. Can Peter bake pies?
B. Of course he can.
He can bake pies very well.

A. Can we speak English?
B. Of course we can.
We can speak English very well.

H WHAT ARE THEY SAYING?

have to	do	don't
has to	does	doesn't

1. Can you play baseball with me?
I'm sorry. I can't. I have to do my homework.
2. Why is Susie upset today?
She ________ ________ go to the dentist this afternoon.
3. Can your husband fix the sink?
No, he can't. He ________ ________ call a plumber.
4. Do I really ________ ________ get a haircut?
Yes, you do. You ________ ________ get a haircut today.
5. ________ Grandma ________ ________ go to the doctor often?
Yes, she ________. She ________ ________ go to the doctor every month.
6. ________ you ________ ________ work today?
No, I ________. I'm on vacation.
7. Do you want to go skiing this weekend?
This weekend? Sorry. We can't. We ________ ________ clean our apartment.
8. Are you bored?
No. I'm tired. I ________ ________ go to bed.

I A BUSY FAMILY

Mr. and Mrs. Lane, their son Danny, and their daughter Julie are very busy this week.

Monday: Dad – speak to the superintendent
Mom – meet with Danny's teacher
Tuesday: Danny and Julie – go to the doctor
Wednesday: Dad – fix the car

Thursday: Mom – go to the dentist
Friday: Julie – baby-sit
Saturday: Mom and Dad – clean the apartment
Danny and Julie – plant flowers in the yard

1. What does Mr. Lane have to do on Monday? He has to speak to the superintendent.
2. What does Mrs. Lane have to do on Monday? ________
3. What do Danny and Julie have to do on Tuesday? ________
4. What does Mr. Lane have to do on Wednesday? ________
5. What does Mrs. Lane have to do on Thursday? ________
6. What does Julie have to do on Friday? ________
7. What do Mr. and Mrs. Lane have to do on Saturday? ________
8. What do Danny and Julie have to do on Saturday? ________

J WRITE ABOUT YOURSELF

What do YOU have to do this week?

....

....

....

....

K LISTENING 

Listen and circle the words you hear.

1.	has to	(have to)	4.	has to	have to	7.	can	can't
2.	has to	have to	5.	can	can't	8.	has to	have to
3.	can	can't	6.	has to	have to	9.	can	can't

L THEY'RE BUSY

can't	baby-sit	go swimming	have dinner
have to	clean the house	go to a movie	study
has to	go bowling	go to a soccer game	wash my clothes
	go dancing	go to the dentist	work

1. I ___can't go swimming___ today.

   I ___have to go the dentist___.

2. Patty ______________ on Saturday.

   She ______________.

3. Bob and Julie ______________ today.

   They ______________.

4. Tom ______________ today.

   He ______________.

5. We ______________ on Saturday.

   We ______________.

6. I ______________ with you today.

   I ______________.

M LISTENING

Listen and choose the correct answer.

1. (a.) She has to go to the dentist.
   b. She can go to the movies.
2. a. He has to wash his car.
   b. He can't go to the party.
3. a. She can have lunch with her friend.
   b. She can have dinner with her friend.
4. a. They have to paint their kitchen.
   b. They can go skiing.
5. a. He has to cook lunch.
   b. He has to go shopping today.
6. a. She has to baby-sit on Friday.
   b. She can't see a play on Saturday.

N GrammarRap: *Where Is Everybody?*

Listen. Then clap and practice.

A. Where's Joe?
B. He has to go.
A. Where's Ray?
B. He can't stay.
A. Where's Kate?
B. She can't wait.
A. Where's Steve?
B. He has to leave.
A. Where's Murray?
B. He has to hurry.
A. What about you?
B. I have to go, too.

All. Oh, no!
Joe has to go.
Ray can't stay.
Kate can't wait.
Steve has to leave.
Murray has to hurry.
What can I do?
I have to go, too.

O GrammarRap: *Can't Talk Now*

Listen. Then clap and practice.

A. I can't talk now.
I have to go to work.
B. I can't stop now.
I have to catch a train.
C. I can't leave now.
I have to make a call.
D. I can't stop now.
I have to catch a plane.

All. She can't stop now.
She has to catch a train.
She can't stop now.
She has to catch a plane.

A WHAT ARE THEY GOING TO DO?

1. What's Larry going to do tomorrow?

He's going to cook.

2. What's Jane going to do tomorrow?

____

3. What are you going to do tomorrow?

____

4. What are they going to do tomorrow?

____

5. What are you and your friends going to do tomorrow?

____

6. What's William going to do tomorrow?

____

B WHAT ARE THEY SAYING?

1. What are you going to do tomorrow?
I'm going to clean my apartment.
3. _______ your mother _______ tomorrow?
_______ plant flowers.

2. _______ your husband _______ tomorrow?
_______ fix the kitchen sink.
4. _______ your cousins _______ tomorrow?
_______ visit us.

C WHAT ARE THEY GOING TO DO?

are	is	going	go	to

1. We're __going__ __to__ __go__ dancing tonight.
2. They're __going__ swimming this afternoon.
3. I'm ______ ______ ______ shopping tomorrow.
4. Brian ______ ______ ______ the library this morning.
5. Rita ______ ______ ______ ______ ______ a party tomorrow night.
6. My friends and I ______ ______ to a baseball game tomorrow afternoon.
7. Mr. and Mrs. Lopez ______ ______ ______ ______ ______ a concert this evening.
8. I'm ______ ______ the supermarket tomorrow morning, and my husband ______ ______ ______ ______ ______ the bank.

D GrammarRap: *What Are You Going to Do?* 

Listen. Then clap and practice.

going to = gonna

All. What are you going to do tomorrow morning?
How about tomorrow afternoon?
What are you going to do tomorrow evening?
What are you going to do this June?

A. I'm going to vacuum all my rugs tomorrow morning.
B. I'm going to walk my dog tomorrow afternoon.
C. I'm going to visit all my friends tomorrow evening.
D. I'm going to dance at my wedding this June.

E WHICH WORD DOESN'T BELONG?

1.	January	May	(Monday)	April
2.	Tuesday	Saturday	Sunday	September
3.	autumn	at once	winter	summer
4.	Friday	February	March	October
5.	him	them	he	her
6.	right now	next week	at once	immediately

F WHAT'S NEXT?

1.	June	July	August	4.	summer	fall	______
2.	Monday	Tuesday	______	5.	Friday	Saturday	______
3.	February	March	______	6.	October	November	______

G MATCH THE SENTENCES

Are you going to . . .

c 1. call your friends on Thursday?

____ 2. fix our doorbell this week?

____ 3. visit your aunt next summer?

____ 4. visit your cousins in April?

____ 5. fix our windows this month?

____ 6. call your uncle this June?

a. No. I'm going to visit them in October.

b. No. I'm going to visit her next winter.

c. No. I'm going to call them on Friday.

d. No. I'm going to fix them next month.

e. No. I'm going to call him this July.

f. No. I'm going to fix it next week.

H LISTENING 

Listen and circle the words you hear.

1.	(this)	next	5.	Tuesday	Thursday	9.	autumn	August
2.	right now	right away	6.	November	December	10.	watch	wash
3.	Monday	Sunday	7.	spring	winter	11.	next	this
4.	wash	cut	8.	at once	next month	12.	number	plumber

I WHAT'S THE QUESTION?

1. We're going to do our exercises right now. What are you going to do right now?
2. She's going to baby-sit this Friday. When ______
3. We're going to Paris next April. Where ______
4. I'm going to clean it because it's dirty. Why ______
5. They're going to go to the beach today. What ______
6. I'm going to fix the doorbell next week. When ______
7. She's going to plant flowers in her yard. Where ______
8. He's going to read his e-mail right now. When ______
9. I'm going to bed now because I'm tired. Why ______

J LISTENING 

Listen to the following weather forecasts and circle the correct answers.

Today's Weather Forecast

This afternoon:	hot	cool	sunny	cloudy
This evening:	foggy	clear	rain	warm

This Weekend's Weather Forecast

Tonight:	cool	cold	clear	warm
Saturday:	cloudy	sunny	foggy	hot
Sunday:	foggy	cool	snow	rain

Monday's Weather Forecast

Monday morning:	cold	cool	cloudy	nice
Monday afternoon:	cool	cold	foggy	snow
Tuesday morning:	sunny	cloudy	nice	warm

K WHAT DOES EVERYBODY WANT TO DO TOMORROW?

want to	wants to

1. I ___want to___ have a picnic tomorrow.
2. George ______________ work in his garden.
3. Karen ______________ take her children to a concert.
4. Mr. and Mrs. Sato ______________ go to the beach.
5. You ______________ see a movie.
6. I ______________ see a play.
7. My friends ______________ go to a basketball game.

L BAD WEATHER

go skiing	go sailing	snow	be cold
take her son to the zoo	go jogging	rain	be warm

1. What does Richard want to do tomorrow?

   ___He wants to go sailing.___

   What's the forecast?

   ___It's going to rain.___

2. What does Lucy want to do this afternoon?

   ____

   What's the forecast?

   ____

3. What do Carl and Betty want to do today?

   ____

   What's the forecast?

   ____

4. What does Jeff want to do tomorrow morning?

   ____

   What's the forecast?

   ____

M YES AND NO

doesn't want to
don't want to

YES! *NO!*

1. My parents want to buy a new car. ___They don't want to buy___ a motorcycle.
2. David wants to go to a baseball game. ______________ to a concert.
3. I want to wash my car. ______________ my clothes.
4. Nancy and Pam want to play baseball. ______________ soccer.
5. Michael wants to cook Italian food. ______________ American food.
6. We want to study English. ______________ history.
7. Margaret wants to dance with John. ______________ with Jim.
8. I want to work in the garden today. ______________ in the kitchen.

N YES AND NO

I'm	not	
He / She / It	isn't	going to
We / You / They	aren't	

1. Steven is going to go swimming. ___He isn't going to go___ sailing.
2. I'm going to take a shower. ______________ a bath.
3. We're going to go bowling. ______________ shopping.
4. Barbara is going to go to the beach. ______________ to the mall.
5. My parents are going to clean the attic. ______________ the basement.
6. It's going to be warm. ______________ cool.
7. Robert is going to listen to the news. ______________ the forecast.
8. You're going to buy a used car. ______________ a new car.

O WHAT DO THEY WANT TO BE?

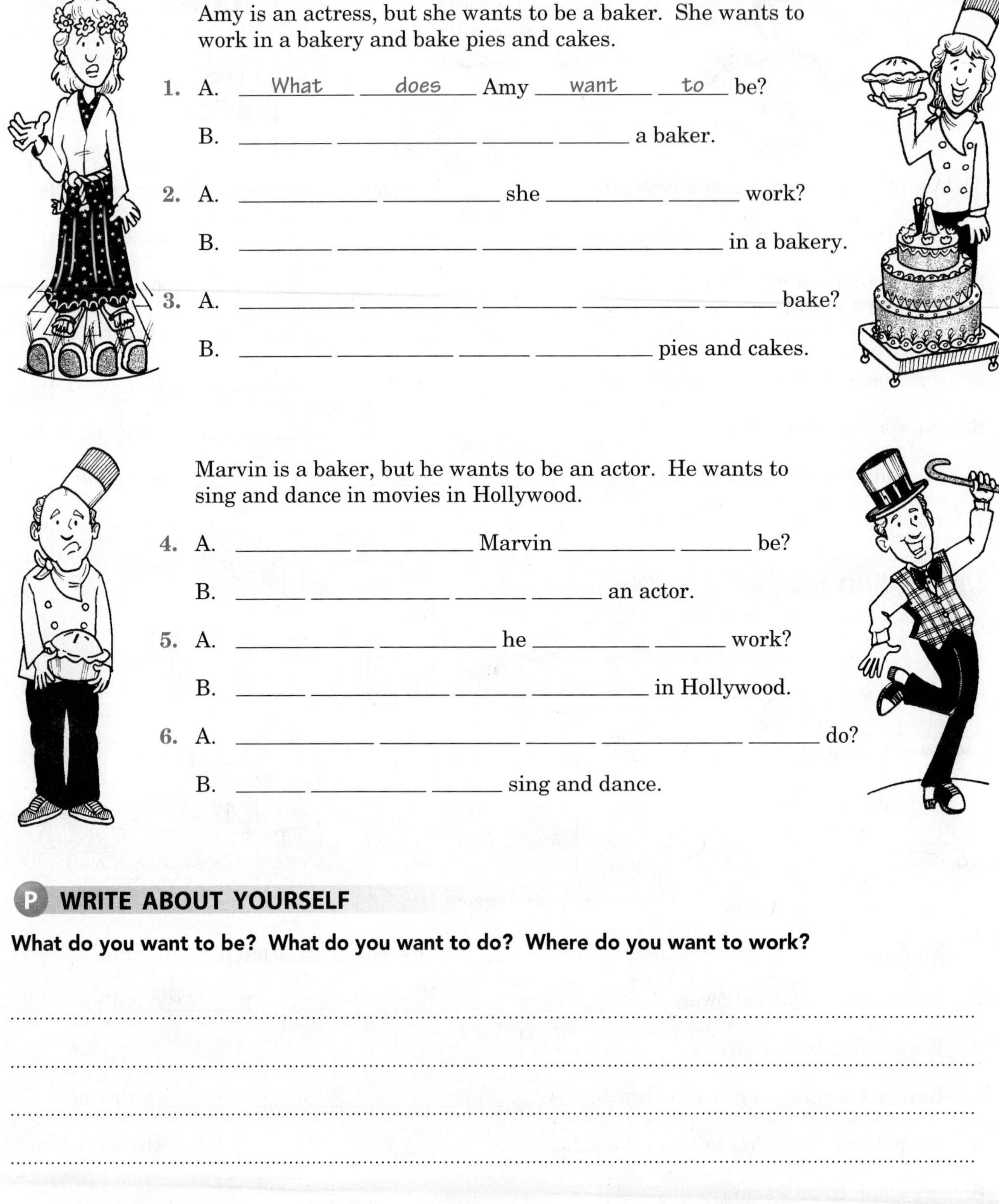

Amy is an actress, but she wants to be a baker. She wants to work in a bakery and bake pies and cakes.

1. A. What does Amy want to be?
   B. ______ ______ ______ ______ a baker.
2. A. ______ ______ she ______ ______ work?
   B. ______ ______ ______ ______ in a bakery.
3. A. ______ ______ ______ ______ ______ bake?
   B. ______ ______ ______ ______ pies and cakes.

Marvin is a baker, but he wants to be an actor. He wants to sing and dance in movies in Hollywood.

4. A. ______ ______ Marvin ______ ______ be?
   B. ______ ______ ______ ______ an actor.
5. A. ______ ______ he ______ ______ work?
   B. ______ ______ ______ ______ in Hollywood.
6. A. ______ ______ ______ ______ ______ do?
   B. ______ ______ ______ sing and dance.

P WRITE ABOUT YOURSELF

What do you want to be? What do you want to do? Where do you want to work?

....

....

....

....

....

....

Q GrammarRap: *What Do They Want to Do?*

Listen. Then clap and practice.

want to = wanna
wants to = wantsta

He wants to go.
I want to stay.
He wants to work.
I want to play.

She wants to eat at a restaurant.
I want to eat at home.
She wants to eat with all our friends.
I want to eat alone.

We want to leave at seven.
They want to leave at eight.
We want to get there early.
They want to get there late.

Jack wants to take the eight o'clock plane.
Joe wants to take the bus.
Bob wants to take the six o'clock train.
Bill wants to come with us.

R WHAT TIME IS IT?

Draw the time on the clocks.

1. It's ten o'clock.

2. It's five fifteen.

3. It's nine thirty.

4. It's three forty-five.

5. It's noon.

6. It's half past eleven.

7. It's a quarter to one.

8. It's a quarter after two.

S WHICH TIMES ARE CORRECT?

Circle the correct times.

1. a. It's four o'clock.
   (b.) It's five o'clock.

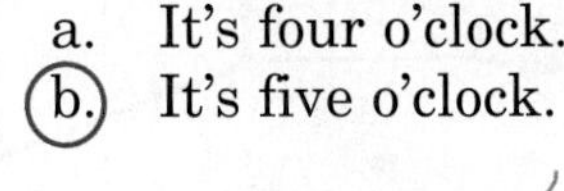

2. a. It's eleven thirteen.
   b. It's eleven thirty.

3. a. It's a quarter after nine.
   b. It's three fifteen.

4. a. It's noon.
   b. It's midnight.

5. a. It's half past six.
   b. It's twelve thirty.

6. a. It's two fifteen.
   b. It's a quarter to three.

7. a. It's one thirty.
   b. It's one forty-five.

8. a. It's a quarter to seven.
   b. It's a quarter after seven.

9. a. It's six o'clock.
   b. It's midnight.

T LISTENING

Listen and write the time you hear.

1. 7:45
2. ______
3. ______
4. ______
5. ______
6. ______
7. ______
8. ______
9. ______
10. ______
11. ______
12. ______

U ALAN CHANG'S DAY

Alan Chang gets up every day at seven fifteen. He brushes his teeth and takes a shower. At seven forty-five he eats breakfast and reads his e-mail. At eight thirty he leaves the house and drives to work. Alan works at a computer company. He begins work at nine o'clock. Every day he uses business software on the computer and talks to people on the telephone. At twelve o'clock Alan is always hungry and thirsty. He eats lunch in the cafeteria. Alan leaves work at five thirty. He eats dinner at six o'clock and then at half past seven he watches videos on his new DVD player.

1. What time does Alan get up every day? He gets up at 7:15.
2. What time does he eat breakfast? ______
3. What time does he leave the house? ______
4. What time does he begin work? ______
5. Where does Alan work? ______
6. What does he do at noon? ______
7. What does he do at half past five? ______
8. What time does he eat dinner? ______
9. What does he do at seven thirty? ______

V YOUR DAY

Answer in complete sentences.

1. What time do you usually get up? ......
2. What do you do after you get up? ......
3. When do you usually leave for school or work? ......
4. What time do you usually have lunch? ......
5. When do you get home from school or work? ......
6. What time do you usually have dinner? ......
7. What do you usually do after dinner? ......
8. When do you usually go to bed? ......

GRAMMARRAP: *Time Flies*

Listen. Then clap and practice.

Time flies.
The days go by.
Monday, Tuesday,
Wednesday, Thursday,
Friday, Saturday.
Time flies.
The days go by.

Time flies.
The months go by.
January, February, March, April,
May, June, July, August,
September, October, November, December.
Time flies.
The months go by.

The seasons come,
The seasons go.
Autumn, winter, spring, summer,
Autumn, winter, spring, summer.
Time flies.
The years go by.
Where do they go?
I don't know.

X GrammarSong: *To Be With You* 

Listen and fill in the words to the song. Then listen again and sing along.

I'm	going	be	after	day	year	December	April	right
it's	wait	in	past	month	fall	February	July	
you	waiting	to	with	week	summer	September		

Any day, any ___week___[1], any month, any ______[2], I'm ______ ______[3] wait right here to be with you.

______[4] the spring, in the ______[5], in the winter, or the ______[6], just call. I'm ______[7] here to be with you.

______ ______[8] to wait from January, ______[9] March, ______[10], May, June and ______[11], August, ______[12], October, and November, and all of ______[13]. I'm going to wait . . .

______[14] one o'clock, a quarter ______[15]. It's half ______[16] one, a quarter ______[17] two. And I'm going ______ ______[18] right here to be with you.

Any ______[19], any week, any ______[20], any year, I'm going to wait ______[21] here to be ______[22] you.

Yes, I'm going to wait right here ______ ______[23] with ______[24].

✓ CHECK-UP TEST: Chapters 13–14

A.

Ex. Ted <u>wants to go skating</u>, but <u>he can't</u>. He <u>has to fix his car</u>.

1. We ______________________, but __________. We ______________________.

2. Alice ______________________, but __________. She ______________________.

3. I ______________________, but __________. I ______________________.

B. Fill in the blanks.

is	are	do	does

Ex. When <u>is</u> Harry going to leave the house?

1. When ________ you going to call the mechanic?
2. ______ you have a bad cold?
3. What ________ they going to do this evening?
4. Where ________ you going skiing?
5. What ________ Carol have to do this Tuesday?
6. ______ your son going to take a bath today?

C. *Ex.* Tom wants to move next spring. <u>He doesn't want to move</u> this fall.

Dad is going to fix the sink. <u>He isn't going to fix</u> the car.

1. I want to teach French. ______________________ English.
2. We're going to bed at 10:00. ______________________ at 9:00.
3. Mrs. Miller can bake pies. ______________________ cakes.
4. Frank has to go to the dentist. ______________________ the doctor.
5. Jim and Julie can speak Japanese. ______________________ Spanish.
6. We have to do our homework. ______________________ our exercises.

D. Every day Helen gets up at 7:30. At 8:00 she eats breakfast, and at 8:30 she goes to work. At noon she has lunch, and at 5:00 she takes the bus home. What's Helen going to do tomorrow?

Tomorrow Helen ______*is going to get up*______ at 7:30. At 8:00 she's ______________[1] breakfast, and at 8:30 ______________[2] to work. At noon ______________[3] lunch, and at 5:00 ______________[4] home.

E. Write the question.

What	When	Where

Ex. I'm going to clean my house this evening. ______*When are you going to clean your house?*______

1. She's going to fix her sink tomorrow. ______________
2. He's going to play tennis in the park. ______________
3. I'm going to go to the zoo this weekend. ______________
4. They're going to study Spanish next year. ______________

F. What time is it?

Ex. It's ten o'clock.

1. It's five fifteen.

2. It's nine thirty.

3. It's noon.

4. It's two forty-five.

5. It's a quarter after eleven.

G. Listen to the story. Fill in the correct times.

English	________	Chinese	________	lunch	________
mathematics	________	science	________	music	________

A TIME ZONES

Read the article on student book page 139 and answer the questions.

SIDE by SIDE Gazette

STUDENT BOOK PAGES **139–140**

1. How many time zones are there around the world?
   a. Twelve
   b. Twenty
   c. Twenty-four
   d. Twenty-five

2. When it's 3:00 in your time zone, what time is it in the time zone to your east?
   a. 2:00
   b. 4:00
   c. 1:00
   d. 5:00

3. When it's 6:30 in your time zone, what time is it in the time zone to your west?
   a. 7:00
   b. 5:00
   c. 7:30
   d. 5:30

4. What time is it in Los Angeles when it's 11:00 in New York?
   a. 10:00
   b. 9:00
   c. 8:00
   d. 7:00

5. When it's noon in New Zealand, what are people doing in London?
   a. They're sleeping.
   b. They're eating lunch.
   c. They're eating breakfast.
   d. They're eating dinner.

6. Which city is an hour ahead of Chicago?
   a. Los Angeles
   b. Denver
   c. New York
   d. London

7. Which city is two hours behind Chicago?
   a. New York
   b. Los Angeles
   c. Denver
   d. London

8. What time is it in New York when it's 11:00 A.M. in Chicago?
   a. 10:00 A.M.
   b. 1:00 P.M.
   c. Midnight
   d. Noon

B BUILD YOUR VOCABULARY!

Choose the job that is right for each person.

____ 1.	Alessandro can use a cash register.	a. painter
____ 2.	Jane wants to work in a restaurant.	b. translator
____ 3.	George can use tools. He likes to fix things.	c. cashier
____ 4.	Josefina can speak three languages fluently.	d. architect
____ 5.	Greta likes to work outdoors.	e. waitress
____ 6.	Sally wants to design buildings.	f. pilot
____ 7.	Bianca can fly airplanes.	g. carpenter
____ 8.	Vladimir can paint houses.	h. farmer

C FACT FILE

Look at the Fact File on student book page 139 and answer the questions.

1. When it's 7:00 A.M. in Mexico City, it's 9:00 P.M. in ______.
   a. Caracas
   b. Lisbon
   c. Hong Kong
   d. Moscow

2. When it's 2:00 P.M. in Madrid, it's also 2:00 P.M. in ______.
   a. Istanbul
   b. Lisbon
   c. Buenos Aires
   d. Rome

3. When it's 5:00 A.M. in Los Angeles, people in Lisbon are ______.
   a. having lunch
   b. having breakfast
   c. going to bed
   d. getting up

4. ______ is two hours ahead of London.
   a. Moscow
   b. Athens
   c. Rome
   d. Rio de Janeiro

5. Istanbul is ______ behind Seoul.
   a. three hours
   b. four hours
   c. seven hours
   d. ten hours

6. When it's 3:00 P.M. in Athens, ______ in Sydney, Australia.
   a. it's noon
   b. it's midnight
   c. people are eating breakfast
   d. people are eating lunch

7. ______ are in the same time zone.
   a. Caracas and Rio de Janeiro
   b. Moscow and Istanbul
   c. Paris and Athens
   d. New York City and Toronto

8. When it's 8:00 A.M. in Toronto, ______.
   a. it's 10:00 A.M. in Seoul
   b. it's 1:00 A.M. in London
   c. it's 2:00 P.M. in Paris
   d. it's 3:00 P.M. in Moscow

D "CAN-DO" REVIEW

Match the "can do" statement and the correct sentence.

____ 1. I can tell my occupation. — a. I'm looking for a job as a chef.

____ 2. I can ask about a person's skills. — b. I have to take a road test.

____ 3. I can tell about my skills. — c. What time is it?

____ 4. I can express my job interests. — d. I'm a construction worker.

____ 5. I can express inability to do something. — e. I'm going to wash my clothes tomorrow.

____ 6. I can express obligation. — f. I can't drive a truck.

____ 7. I can give the time. — g. What's the forecast?

____ 8. I can tell about future plans. — h. I can use business software.

____ 9. I can ask about the weather. — i. It's four o'clock.

____ 10. I can ask the time. — j. Can you type?

STUDENT BOOK
PAGES **141–148**

A WHAT'S THE MATTER?

backache	cough	fever	sore throat	toothache
cold	earache	headache	stomachache	

1. He  has a cold ______________.
2. She ______________ ______________.
3. I ______________ ______________.

4. She ______________ ______________.
5. I ______________ ______________.
6. He ______________ ______________.

7. She ______________ ______________.
8. You ______________ ______________.
9. He ______________ ______________.

 LISTENING 

Listen to the story. Put the number under the correct picture.

______

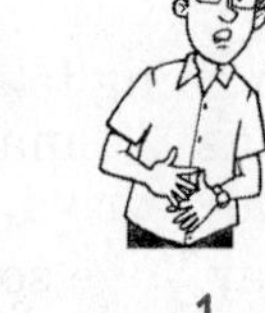

__1__

______

______

______

______

______

______

C GrammarRap: *What's the Matter?* 

Listen. Then clap and practice.

A. What's the matter with you?
B. I have a headache.
What's the matter with YOU?
A. I have a cold.

A. What's the matter with him?
B. He has a toothache.
What's the matter with HER?
A. She has a cold.

A. What's the matter with Mary?
B. She has an earache.
What's the matter with BILL?
A. He has a very bad cold.

A. What's the matter with Fred?
B. He has a backache.
What's the matter with ANNE?
A. She has an awful cold.

A. What's the matter with Jane?
B. She has a stomachache.
What's the matter with PAUL?
A. He has a terrible cold.

A. What's the matter with the students?
B. They have sore throats.
What's the matter with the teachers?
A. They have terrible colds.
They have terrible terrible colds!

D WHAT DID YOU DO YESTERDAY?

bake	cook	dance	rest	shout	study
clean	cry	paint	shave	smile	type

1. I ___cooked___.
2. I ________.
3. I ________.

4. I ________.
5. I ________.
6. I ________.

7. I ________.
8. I ________.
9. I ________.

10. I ________.
11. I ________.
12. I ________.

E WHAT'S THE WORD?

brush	cook	paint	plant	play	study	wait	watch	work

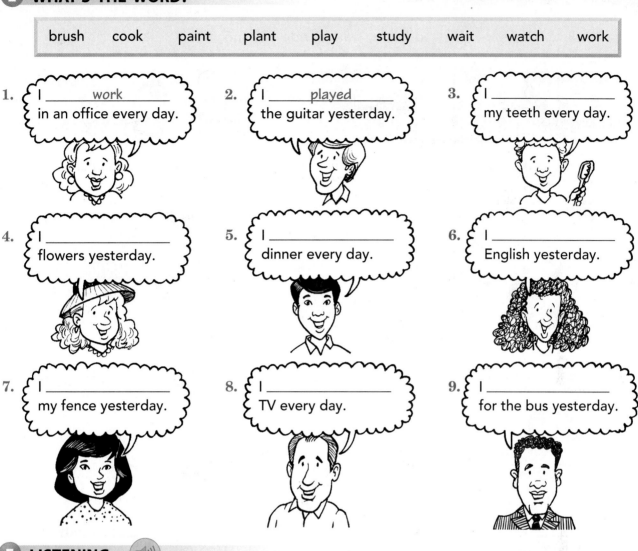

1. I ___work___ in an office every day.
2. I ___played___ the guitar yesterday.
3. I __________ my teeth every day.
4. I __________ flowers yesterday.
5. I __________ dinner every day.
6. I __________ English yesterday.
7. I __________ my fence yesterday.
8. I __________ TV every day.
9. I __________ for the bus yesterday.

F LISTENING

Listen and circle the correct answer.

Ex. I study.

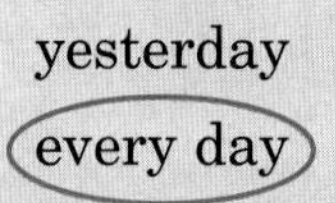

yesterday / (every day)

I played cards.

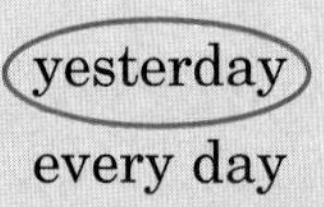

(yesterday) / every day

1.	yesterday every day	4.	yesterday every day	7.	yesterday every day	10.	yesterday every day
2.	yesterday every day	5.	yesterday every day	8.	yesterday every day	11.	yesterday every day
3.	yesterday every day	6.	yesterday every day	9.	yesterday every day	12.	yesterday every day

G WHAT DID EVERYBODY DO?

bark	clean	cry	drink	eat	ride	sing	sit	skate	write

1. A. What did James do today?

   B. ___He cleaned___ his apartment all day.

2. A. What did your sister do today?

   B. ______________ letters all morning.

3. A. What did Mr. and Mrs. Porter do yesterday?

   B. ______________ songs all evening.

4. A. What did you and your friends do today?

   B. ______________ in the park all afternoon.

5. A. What did Linda do yesterday?

   B. ______________ lemonade all morning.

6. A. What did Jimmy do today?

   B. ______________ candy and cookies all day.

7. A. What did Mrs. Mason's children do today?

   B. ______________ all afternoon.

8. A. What did the neighbors' dogs do yesterday?

   B. ______________ all night.

9. A. What did Howard do yesterday?

   B. ______________ in the clinic all evening.

10. A. What did Grandma do today?

    B. ______________ her bicycle all afternoon.

H PUZZLE

Across

3. ride
4. study
6. eat

Down

1. cry
2. work
4. sit
5. drink

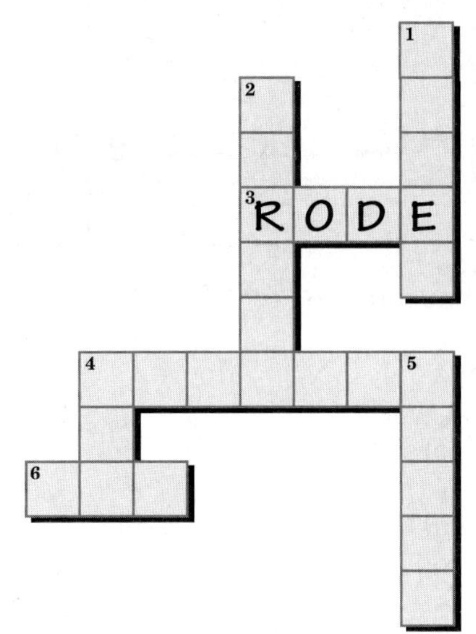

I PETER'S DAY AT HOME

bake	cook	fix	paint	plant	rest	wash

1. Thank you, Peter. This is a very good dinner.
3. Look at the car! It's really clean. Thank you.
5. The kitchen looks beautiful. Yellow is my favorite color.

2. This is a wonderful cake, Peter.
4. The new flowers in the garden are beautiful.
6. The sink isn't broken! I can brush my teeth in the bathroom now!

What did Peter do today?

1. He cooked dinner.
2. ______
3. ______
4. ______
5. ______
6. ______

What did Peter do after dinner?

7. ______

J GRAMMARRAP: *What Did They Do?*

Listen. Then clap and practice.

washed [t]	cleaned [d]	painted [ɪd]

A. What did you do today?
B. I washed my floors.
A. Your floors? B. Yes!
B. I washed my floors all day!

A. What did Mark do today?
B. He cleaned his house.
A. His house? B. Yes!
B. He cleaned his house all day!

A. What did Pam do today?
B. She painted her porch.
A. Her porch? B. Yes!
B. She painted her porch all day!

A. What did they do today?
B. They sang some songs.
A. Some songs? B. Yes!
They sang some songs all day!

A. What did you do today?
B. I ________________________.
A. ____________? B. Yes!
B. I ________________________ all day!

K MY GRANDFATHER'S BIRTHDAY PARTY

At my grandfather's birthday party last night, everybody (listen) ___listened___ [1] to Mexican music and (dance) ______________ [2]. My sister Gloria (sing) ______________ [3] my grandfather's favorite songs all evening, and my brother Daniel (play) ______________ [4] the guitar.

Everybody (sit) ______________ [5] in the living room with my grandmother and grandfather and (look) ______________ [6] at old photographs. We (laugh) ______________ [7], we (smile) ______________ [8], we (cry) ______________ [9], and we (talk) ______________ [10] about "the good old days." What did I do at my grandfather's birthday party? I (drink) ______________ [11] lemonade and (eat) ______________ [12] a lot of food!

L MATCHING

_e_	1. At the party my brother played ______.	a.	drank lemonade all night
____	2. Everybody sat and talked about ______.	b.	Mexican music
____	3. My sister has a sore throat today because ______.	c.	"the good old days"
____	4. We all looked at ______.	d.	ate a lot of food
____	5. We listened to ______.	e.	the guitar
____	6. I have a toothache today because I ______.	f.	old photographs
____	7. I also have a stomachache because I ______.	g.	she sang all evening

A CORRECT THE SENTENCE

STUDENT BOOK
PAGES **149–156**

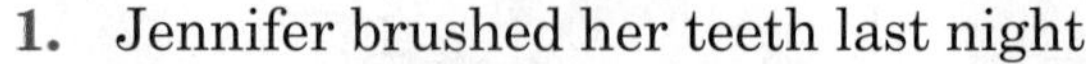

1. Jennifer brushed her teeth last night.

   She didn't brush her teeth.

   She brushed her hair.

2. Kevin played the violin yesterday afternoon.

   ____

   ____

3. Harold and Betty listened to the news yesterday evening.

   ____

   ____

4. Mrs. Martinez waited for the train this afternoon.

   ____

   ____

5. Frank fixed his fence yesterday morning.

   ____

   ____

6. Mr. and Mrs. Park cleaned their attic today.

   ____

   ____

7. Marvin baked a pie yesterday evening.

   ____

   ____

8. Patty called her grandmother last night.

   ____

   ____

B ALAN AND HIS SISTER

Alan and his sister Ellen did very different things yesterday. Alan (rest) ___rested___¹ all day. He didn't (work) ________², and he didn't (study) ________³. He (listen) ________⁴ to music yesterday morning. He (watch) ________⁵ game shows on TV yesterday afternoon. And yesterday evening he (talk) ________⁶ to his friends on the telephone and (play) ________⁷ games on his computer.

Ellen didn't (listen) ________⁸ to music. She didn't (watch) ________⁹ game shows on TV, and she didn't (play) ________¹⁰ games on her computer. What did she do? She (study) ________¹¹ English yesterday morning. She (clean) ________¹² the yard yesterday afternoon. And she (cook) ________¹³ dinner for her family last night.

C YES AND NO

1. Did Alan rest all day yesterday? ___Yes, he did.___
2. Did Ellen rest all day yesterday? ___No, she didn't.___
3. Did Ellen study yesterday morning? ________
4. Did Alan study yesterday morning? ________
5. Did Alan watch TV yesterday afternoon? ________

6. ___Did Ellen clean___ the yard yesterday afternoon? Yes, she did.
7. ________ to his friends yesterday evening? Yes, he did.
8. ________ dinner for his family last night? No, he didn't.
9. ________ to music yesterday morning? No, she didn't.
10. ________ game shows yesterday afternoon? No, she didn't.
11. ________ English yesterday afternoon? No, he didn't.

D WHAT DID THEY DO?

1. I didn't buy a car. I ___bought___ a motorcycle.
2. Michael didn't have a headache. He __________ a toothache.
3. Alice didn't write to her uncle. She __________ to her cousin.
4. We didn't do our homework last night. We __________ yoga.
5. They didn't take the bus to work today. They __________ the train.
6. Barbara didn't get up at 7:00 this morning. She __________ up at 6:00.
7. My friend and I didn't go swimming yesterday. We __________ bowling.
8. Martha didn't read the newspaper last night. She __________ a book.
9. My children didn't make breakfast this morning. They __________ lunch.

E THEY DIDN'T DO WHAT THEY USUALLY DO

1.	Robert usually writes to his friends.	He ___didn't___ ___write___ to his friends yesterday.	He ___wrote___ to his grandparents.
2.	I usually have a cold in January.	I ________ ________ a cold last January.	I ________ a cold last July.
3.	We usually eat at home on Friday night.	We ________ ________ at home last Friday night.	We ________ at a very nice restaurant.
4.	Bill usually gets up 7:00 o'clock.	He ________ ________ up at 7:00 this morning.	He ________ up at 10:00.
5.	Tom and Tina usually go dancing every week.	They ________ ________ dancing this week.	They ________ sailing.
6.	Susie usually drinks milk every afternoon.	She ________ ________ milk this afternoon.	She ________ lemonade.
7.	My brother usually makes lunch on Sunday.	He ________ ________ lunch last Sunday.	He ________ dinner.
8.	Mr. Lee usually takes his wife to the movies.	He ________ ________ his wife to the movies last night.	He ________ his daughter and his son-in-law.
9.	We usually buy food at a large supermarket.	We ________ ________ food at a supermarket today.	We ________ food at a small grocery store.
10.	I usually sit next to Maria in English class.	I ________ ________ next to Maria yesterday.	I ________ next to her sister Carmen.

F GrammarRap Rhyming Game: *No, They Didn't*

A. Did she wash her skirt?
B. No, she didn't.
A. What did she wash?
B. She washed her shirt.

A. Did they paint the door?
B. No, they didn't.
A. What did they paint?
B. They painted the ________.

A. Did he call his mother?
B. No, he didn't.
A. Who did he call?
B. He called his ________.

A. Did you buy new suits?
B. No, we didn't.
A. What did you buy?
B. We bought new ________.

A. Did you get up at seven?
B. No, I didn't.
A. When did you get up?
B. I got up at ________.

G WHAT'S THE ANSWER?

1. Did Henry ride his bicycle to work this morning? Yes, he did.
2. Did you get up at 6:00 this morning? No, ________.
3. Did your sister call you last night? Yes, ________.
4. Did Mr. and Mrs. Chen clean their apartment last weekend? No, ________.
5. Did you and your friends go to the library yesterday afternoon? Yes, ________.
6. Did your father make spaghetti for dinner last night? No, ________.
7. Excuse me. Did I take your gloves? Yes, ________.
8. Bob, did you do your exercises today? No, ________.

H WHAT'S THE QUESTION?

1. Did she buy a car? No, she didn't. She bought a truck.
2. ________ a headache? No, he didn't. He had a backache.
3. ________ a shower? No, I didn't. I took a bath.
4. ________ to the supermarket? No, they didn't. They went to the bank.
5. ________ in the living room? No, we didn't. We sat in the kitchen.
6. ________ a right turn? No, you didn't. You made a left turn.

I LISTENING

Listen and choose the correct response.

1. a. I write to her every day.
   (b.) I wrote to her this morning.
2. a. He washes it every weekend.
   b. He washed it last weekend.
3. a. They visit my aunt and my uncle.
   b. They visited my aunt and my uncle.
4. a. She did yoga in the park.
   b. She does yoga in the park.
5. a. He went to sleep at 8:00.
   b. He goes to sleep at 8:00.
6. a. We clean it every weekend.
   b. We cleaned it last weekend.
7. a. We take them to the zoo.
   b. We took them to the zoo.
8. a. I make spaghetti.
   b. I made spaghetti.
9. a. She reads it every afternoon.
   b. She read it this afternoon.
10. a. I get up at 7:00.
    b. I got up at 7:00.

J I'M SORRY I'M LATE!

forget	go	have to	miss
get up	have	meet	steal

1. I ___missed___ the train.

2. I ________________ a headache.

3. I ________________ my lunch.

4. I ________________ my girlfriend on the way to work.

5. I ________________ late.

6. A thief ________________ my bicycle.

7. I ________________ go to the bank.

8. I ________________ to sleep on the bus.

K MATCHING

_d_	1. buy	a.	wrote	____	7. get	g.	had
____	2. steal	b.	did	____	8. eat	h.	drove
____	3. do	c.	went	____	9. have	i.	made
____	4. see	d.	bought	____	10. forget	j.	got
____	5. go	e.	saw	____	11. make	k.	forgot
____	6. write	f.	stole	____	12. drive	l.	ate

L GrammarRap: *Old Friends* 

Listen. Then clap and practice.

We walked and talked
And talked and walked.
Walked and talked,
Talked and walked.

We sat in the garden
And looked at the flowers.
We talked and talked
For hours and hours.

He drank milk,
And I drank tea.
We talked and talked
From one to three.

We talked about him.
We talked about us.
Then we walked to the corner
To get the bus.

We waited and waited.
The bus was late.
So we stood and talked
From four to eight.

M GrammarRap: *Gossip* 

Listen. Then clap and practice.

I told Jack.
Jack told Jill.
Jill told Fred.
Fred told Bill.
Bill called Anne.
Anne called Sue.
Sue told Jim.
But who told you?

17

STUDENT BOOK
PAGES **157–164**

A A TERRIBLE DAY AND A WONDERFUL DAY

was	were

We ___were___ 1 very upset at work last Friday. Our computers ________ 2 broken, our boss ________ 3 angry because he ________ 4 tired, and my friends and I ________ 5 sick. Outside it ________ 6 cloudy and it ________ 7 very cold. And then in the afternoon all the trains ________ 8 late. I ________ 9 hungry when I got home, and my children ________ 10 very noisy. It ________ 11 a terrible day!

We ___were___ 12 very happy at work on Monday. Our computers ________ 13 fine, our boss ________ 14 happy, and my friends and I ________ 15 energetic. Outside it ________ 16 sunny, it ________ 17 warm, and all the trains ________ 18 early. My children ________ 19 very quiet when I got home. We ate a big dinner, and I ________ 20 very full. It was a wonderful day!

B LISTENING

Listen and circle the word you hear.

1.	(is) / was	4.	is / was	7.	are / were	10.	is / was
2.	is / was	5.	is / was	8.	are / were	11.	are / were
3.	are / were	6.	are / were	9.	is / was	12.	are / were

C BEFORE AND AFTER

clean	enormous	happy	shiny	thin
comfortable	full	healthy	tall	

1. Before I took A-1 Vitamins, I ___was___ always sick. Now ___I'm___ ___healthy___.

2. Before Harold met Gertrude, he ________ sad. Now ________ ______________ all the time.

3. Before we ate a big breakfast today, we __________ hungry. Now __________ __________.

4. Before Helen got her new sofa, she ________ uncomfortable. Now ________ very __________________.

5. Before you drank A-1 Skim Milk, you __________ heavy. Now __________ __________.

6. Before Charlie used A-1 Car Wax, his car __________ dull. Now ________ ______________.

7. Before these children used A-1 soap, they __________ dirty. Now ____________ ____________.

8. When I __________ young, I __________ very short. Now __________ __________.

9. Before we bought A-1 Bird Food, our birds __________ very tiny. Now ____________ ________________.

D WHAT'S THE WORD?

1. A. ___Were___ you at a concert last night?

   B. No, I ___wasn't___. I ___was___ at a play.

2. A. __________ your neighbors quiet last Saturday night?

   B. No, they __________. They __________ very noisy.

3. A. __________ your boss in the office yesterday?

   B. No, she __________. She __________ on vacation.

4. A. __________ we at home last Tuesday?

   B. No, we __________. We __________ at the mall.

5. A. __________ the questions on the examination easy?

   B. No, they __________. They __________ very difficult.

6. A. __________ Timothy on time for his wedding?

   B. No, he __________. He __________ late.

E LISTENING

Listen and circle the word you hear.

1.	was / (wasn't)	3.	were / weren't	5.	was / wasn't	7.	were / weren't
2.	were / weren't	4.	was / wasn't	6.	were / weren't	8.	was / wasn't

F WHAT'S THE WORD?

did	was	were
didn't	wasn't	weren't

A. Why ___did___ 1 Victor leave the party early?

B. He ________ 2 like the party. It ________ 3 noisy, the food ________ 4 very good, and his friends ________ 5 there.

A. Where ________ 6 you last week? You ________ 7 at work.

B. That's right. I ________ 8.

A. ________ 9 you sick?

B. Yes, I ________ 10. I ________ 11 very sick. I had an earache and a cold.

A. ________ 12 you also have a headache?

B. No. I ________ 13 have a headache, but I had a sore throat. I ________ 14 go to work all week. I ________ 15 really sick!

A. How ________ 16 your vacation?

B. It ________ 17 terrible!

A. That's too bad. ________ 18 you like the hotel?

B. No, we ________ 19. The bathroom sink ________ 20 broken, the hotel room ________ 21 clean, and we ________ 22 sleep well at night because the people in the next room ________ 23 very loud.

A. ________ 24 you swim at the beach?

B. No, we ________ 25. The weather ________ 26 very cold!

A. ________ 27 your grandchildren visit you last weekend?

B. No, they ________ 28.

A. That's too bad. ________ 29 they busy?

B. My grandson ________ 30 feel well, and my granddaughter ________ 31 on a business trip. We ________ 32 sad because we ________ 33 see them.

G GrammarRap: *Were You Late This Morning?*

Listen. Then clap and practice.

A. Were you late this morning?
B. No, I wasn't. I was early.
A. Was he sick last night?
B. No, he wasn't. He was fine.
A. Was her hair very straight?
B. No, it wasn't. It was curly.
A. Were there eight new lessons?
B. No, there weren't. There were nine.

A. Was the movie short?
B. No, it wasn't. It was long.
A. Was the food expensive?
B. No, it wasn't. It was free.
A. Was I right?
B. No, you weren't. You were wrong.
A. Were the tickets two dollars?
B. No, they weren't. They were three.

H WHAT ARE THEY SAYING?

basketball	did	freckles	short	subjects	wasn't	weren't
curly	didn't	hobby	sports	was	were	

A. Tell me, what ___did___ 1 you look like when you _______ 2 young? _______ 3 you tall?

B. No, I _______ 4. I _______ 5 _______ 6.

A. _______ 7 you have straight hair?

B. No, I _______ 8. I had _______ 9 hair.

A. Oh. And _______ 10 you have dimples?

B. No, I _______ 11, but I had _______ 12.

A. I'm sure you _______ 13 very cute!

What _______ 14 you do with your friends?

B. We played sports.

A. Oh. What _______ 15 you play?

B. We played _______ 16 and tennis.

A. Tell me, _______ 17 you like school?

B. Yes. I liked school a lot.

A. What _______ 18 your favorite _______ 19?

B. English and mathematics.

A. _______ 20 you have a _______ 21?

B. Yes, I _______ 22. I played chess.

I LISTENING

Listen and choose the correct response.

1. a. I was born last week.
   (b.) I was born in Japan.
2. a. Yes, I did.
   b. I grew up in Tokyo.
3. a. English.
   b. No, I didn't.
4. a. In Los Angeles.
   b. Last year.

5. a. I was tall and thin.
   b. I didn't look.
6. a. No. I had straight hair.
   b. No. I had dimples.
7. a. I played sports.
   b. I play chess.
8. a. Yes. I'm here.
   b. Yes. My father.

J GrammarRap: *The Teacher Was There* 

Listen. Then clap and practice.

A. The teacher was there,
But where were the students?
B. The students were there.
All. Where?

A. The teacher was there,
The students were there,
But where were the books?
B. The books were there.
All. Where?

A. The teacher was there,
The students were there,
The books were there,
But where was the chalk?
B. The chalk was there.
All. Where?

A. The teacher was there,
The students were there,
The books were there,
The chalk was there,
But where were the chairs?
B. The chairs were there.
All. Where?
B. There.
All. Where?
B. Right there!
Right there!

✓ CHECK-UP TEST: Chapters 15–17

A. Fill in the blanks.

was	were	wasn't	weren't

1. A. ___Was___ Barbara at work yesterday?
   B. No, she __________. She __________ sick.
2. A. Why __________ you late today?
   B. I __________ late because I __________ on time for the bus.
3. A. Where __________ Grandma and Grandpa last night? They __________ at home.
   B. They __________ at a concert.

B. Complete the sentences.

Ex. Before we washed our car, it ___was___ dirty. Now ___it's___ ___clean___.

1. Before I ate dinner, I __________ hungry. Now __________ __________.
2. When I got my cats, they __________ tiny. Now __________ __________.
3. When we __________ in college, we __________ thin. Now __________ __________.
4. When I was young, I __________ energetic. Now __________ __________.

C. Complete the sentences.

Ex. a. Carla usually studies English.	She ___didn't___ ___study___ English yesterday.	She ___studied___ mathematics.
b. Paul usually writes to his friends.	He ___didn't___ ___write___ to his friends yesterday.	He ___wrote___ to his cousins.
1. I usually drive to the park on Saturday.	I __________ __________ to the park last Saturday.	I __________ to the mall.
2. We usually arrive late.	We __________ __________ late today.	We __________ on time.
3. My husband and my son usually shave in the morning.	They __________ __________ in the morning today.	They __________ in the afternoon.
4. Bob usually goes jogging in the evening.	He __________ __________ jogging yesterday evening.	He __________ dancing.
5. Margaret usually reads the newspaper in the morning.	She __________ __________ the newspaper yesterday morning.	She __________ a magazine.

D. Write the question.

Ex. ___Did they get up___ at 8:00? — No, they didn't. They got up at 10:00.

1. ______________________ his brother? — No, he didn't. He met his sister.
2. ______________________ her bicycle? — No, she didn't. She rode her motorcycle.
3. ______________________ a good time? — No, we didn't. We had a terrible time.
4. ______________________ lunch? — No, they didn't. They made dinner.
5. ______________________ a movie? — No, I didn't. I saw a play.

E. Read the story and then write about yesterday.

Every morning I get up early. I brush my teeth, and I do my exercises. Then I sit in the kitchen and I eat breakfast. At 8:00 I go to work. I walk to the drug store and I buy a newspaper. Then I take the train to my office. I don't take the bus, and I don't drive my car.

Yesterday I ___got up___ early. I __________[1] my teeth, and I __________[2] my exercises. Then I __________[3] in the kitchen and I __________[4] breakfast. At 8:00 I __________[5] to work. I __________[6] to the drug store and I __________[7] a newspaper. Then I __________[8] the train to my office. I __________ __________[9] the bus, and I __________ __________[10] my car.

F. Listen and circle the word you hear.

Ex.	(is) / was	3.	is / was	6.	are / were
1.	is / was	4.	are / were	7.	is / was
2.	are / were	5.	is / was	8.	are / were

A ADVERTISEMENTS

SIDE by SIDE Gazette

STUDENT BOOK PAGES 165–166

Read the article on student book page 165 and answer the questions.

1. You can hear advertisements ______.
   a. on top of taxis
   b. in newspapers
   c. on the radio
   d. in magazines

2. An unusual place for an advertisement is ______.
   a. on a bus
   b. in an elevator
   c. in the mail
   d. on the Internet

3. You can find advertisements everywhere because advertisers want to ______.
   a. make products
   b. buy products
   c. sell products
   d. use products

4. The main idea of the article is ______.
   a. advertisements are a problem
   b. advertisements are unusual
   c. advertisements are interesting
   d. advertisements are everywhere

5. The article does NOT talk about advertisements in ______.
   a. movie theaters
   b. shopping malls
   c. public bathrooms
   d. the sky

6. You often see advertisements on billboards when you are ______.
   a. reading the mail
   b. driving on the highway
   c. shopping at the supermarket
   d. looking at a magazine

B BUILD YOUR VOCABULARY! What's the Word?

Write the correct word.

closed	dark	fast	high	light	long	messy	plain	wet

1. Clean your room! It's very ____________________. There are papers everywhere.
2. Roland was out in the rain all afternoon. His clothes are very ____________________.
3. The library is open on weekdays, but it's ____________________ on weekends.
4. At midnight it's very ____________________ outside.
5. I can carry the sign. It's very ____________________.
6. I have to go to the barber. My hair is very ____________________.
7. Alicia always finishes her work before the other students. She's very ____________________.
8. I can't see the house because there's a very ____________________ wall in front of it.
9. I don't want a dress with flowers on it. I'm looking for something ____________________.

C BUILD YOUR VOCABULARY! Crossword

Across

3. The store isn't closed. It's ______.
4. Their fence isn't high. It's ______.
5. Her blouse isn't plain. It's ______.
7. His hair isn't long. It's ______.

Down

1. Our car isn't fast. It's ______.
2. That suitcase isn't light. It's ______.
6. My room isn't messy. It's ______

3 OPEN

D FACT FILE

Look at the Fact File on student book page 165. Write the countries in alphabetical order.

Australia, ______________________________

____

E "CAN-DO" REVIEW

Match the "can do" statement and the correct sentence.

____ 1.	I can describe my health.	a.	I have to do my homework.
____ 2.	I can ask about a person's health.	b.	What did you do yesterday?
____ 3.	I can ask about past activities.	c.	I was happy.
____ 4.	I can tell about past activities.	d.	I recommend *Presto* Floor Wax.
____ 5.	I can apologize for something.	e.	I have a fever.
____ 6.	I can tell about obligation.	f.	Can you recommend a good restaurant?
____ 7.	I can describe my feelings and emotions.	g.	I'm sorry I'm late.
____ 8.	I can express sympathy.	h.	How do you feel today?
____ 9.	I can ask for a recommendation.	i.	I'm sorry to hear that.
____ 10.	I can give a recommendation.	j.	I washed my car yesterday.

CHECK-UP TESTS SKILLS CHECKS

Choose the correct answer.

1. Where ____?
   (A) you live
   (B) you do live
   (C) do you live
   (D) live you

2. What language ____?
   (A) he speaks
   (B) do he speak
   (C) he does speak
   (D) does he speak

3. We're Carol and Dan. ____ in London.
   (A) We work
   (B) They work
   (C) We works
   (D) Do we work

4. Carla ____ the newspaper every day.
   (A) read
   (B) does she read
   (C) she read
   (D) reads

5. What ____ every day?
   (A) you do
   (B) do you do
   (C) do you
   (D) does you do

6. I'm from Canada. I speak ____.
   (A) Canadian
   (B) Toronto
   (C) English and French
   (D) language

7. We eat Mexican ____ every day.
   (A) music
   (B) food
   (C) shopping malls
   (D) songs

8. I ____ my grandparents every weekend.
   (A) visit
   (B) listen
   (C) paint
   (D) speak

9. My sister ____ a bus.
   (A) works
   (B) talks
   (C) calls
   (D) drives

10. My husband ____ cars.
    (A) plays
    (B) sells
    (C) lives
    (D) reads

SKILLS CHECK 

Match the "can do" statement and the correct sentence.

____	1. I can ask a person's name.	a.	I'm Greek.
____	2. I can tell where I live.	b.	What does she do?
____	3. I can tell what language I speak.	c.	Hmm. Well, . . .
____	4. I can tell about my nationality.	d.	I live in Seoul.
____	5. I can tell about my work.	e.	He's sad.
____	6. I can ask about a person's work.	f.	What's your name?
____	7. I can describe a person's emotions.	g.	I drive a taxi.
____	8. I can hesitate while I'm thinking.	h.	I speak Spanish.

Choose the correct answer.

1. ____ Michael ____ Italian food?
   Ⓐ Does . . . likes
   Ⓑ Do . . . like
   Ⓒ Does . . . like
   Ⓓ Do . . . likes

2. ____ your parents ____ English?
   Ⓐ Does . . . speak
   Ⓑ Do . . . speaks
   Ⓒ Are . . . speak
   Ⓓ Do . . . speak

3. A. Does your sister play tennis?
   B. Yes, ____.
   Ⓐ she doesn't
   Ⓑ she does
   Ⓒ she do
   Ⓓ does she

4. A. Do your friends sing in the choir?
   B. No, ____.
   Ⓐ do they
   Ⓑ don't they
   Ⓒ they don't
   Ⓓ they do

5. Bob ____ work on Saturday. He ____ on Sunday.
   Ⓐ doesn't . . . works
   Ⓑ does . . . work
   Ⓒ don't . . . work
   Ⓓ does . . . works

6. I ride ____ every day.
   Ⓐ American food
   Ⓑ a different kind of sport
   Ⓒ books
   Ⓓ my bicycle

7. My daughter plays ____.
   Ⓐ a musical instrument
   Ⓑ karate
   Ⓒ dinner
   Ⓓ novels

8. I work during the week. I don't work on the weekend. I don't work on ____.
   Ⓐ Tuesday
   Ⓑ Sunday
   Ⓒ Thursday
   Ⓓ Monday

9. I read every day. I usually read ____.
   Ⓐ videos
   Ⓑ game shows
   Ⓒ classical music
   Ⓓ short stories

10. Janet is very athletic. She ____ every weekend.
   Ⓐ sings
   Ⓑ plays in the orchestra
   Ⓒ plays tennis
   Ⓓ sees a play

SKILLS CHECK 

Match the "can do" statement and the correct sentence.

____ **1.** I can say the days of the week.
____ **2.** I can talk about work activities.
____ **3.** I can talk about likes.
____ **4.** I can talk about dislikes.
____ **5.** I can describe recreational activities.
____ **6.** I can describe people.
____ **7.** I can start a conversation.
____ **8.** I can ask questions to make small talk.

a. I like Chinese food.
b. On Sunday I ride my bike.
c. Sheldon is a very shy person.
d. Mr. Garcia works at the post office.
e. Tell me, . . .
f. What kind of movies do you like?
g. Sunday, Monday, Tuesday, . . .
h. I don't like American food.

Choose the correct answer.

1. I ____ long hair and my brother ____ short hair.
   - (A) has . . . has
   - (B) have . . . has
   - (C) have . . . have
   - (D) has . . . have

2. A. How often do you see your neighbor?
   B. I see ____ every day.
   - (A) them
   - (B) us
   - (C) her
   - (D) me

3. A. How often do your cousins visit you?
   B. They visit ____ every summer.
   - (A) them
   - (B) him
   - (C) her
   - (D) us

4. I often ____ TV. My wife rarely ____ it.
   - (A) watch . . . watch
   - (B) watches . . . watches
   - (C) watch . . . watches
   - (D) watches . . . watch

5. Mr. DeLuca is ____ landlord. I like ____ very much.
   - (A) my . . . him
   - (B) our . . . her
   - (C) your . . . them
   - (D) my . . . us

6. Marie ____ her computer every day.
   - (A) writes
   - (B) reads
   - (C) uses
   - (D) makes

7. I usually take the bus to work. I ____.
   - (A) always drive
   - (B) usually drive
   - (C) drive every day
   - (D) rarely drive

8. I wash my car every Sunday. I wash it ____.
   - (A) once a day
   - (B) once a week
   - (C) once a month
   - (D) once a year

9. My son has ____ eyes.
   - (A) curly
   - (B) blue
   - (C) blond
   - (D) tall

10. We never go out on the weekend. We always ____.
    - (A) go to the movies
    - (B) go to parties
    - (C) go dancing
    - (D) watch videos at home

SKILLS CHECK

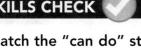

Match the "can do" statement and the correct sentence.

____ 1. I can talk about everyday activities.
____ 2. I can tell about family members.
____ 3. I can describe people.
____ 4. I can give my occupation.
____ 5. I can give my marital status.
____ 6. I can compare myself with another person.
____ 7. I can ask for information.
____ 8. I can react to information.

a. I'm a journalist.
b. Linda usually eats in the cafeteria.
c. Oh, really? That's interesting.
d. I'm single.
e. We're very different.
f. He has long, straight hair.
g. Tell me about your sister.
h. Our grandchildren call us every Sunday.

Choose the correct answer.

1. ____ a big breakfast today because she's very hungry.
   (A) She has
   (B) She's having
   (C) She doesn't have
   (D) She isn't having

2. ____ because I'm angry. I always ____ when I'm angry.
   (A) I shout . . . shouting
   (B) I'm shouting . . . shouting
   (C) I'm shouting . . . shout
   (D) I shouting . . . shout

3. I never ____ to work, but ____ to work today.
   (A) walk . . . I walk
   (B) walking . . . I'm walking
   (C) walking . . . I walk
   (D) walk . . . I'm walking

4. Why ____ today? He hardly ever ____.
   (A) is he smiling . . . smiles
   (B) he smiles . . . smiles
   (C) does he smile . . . is smiling
   (D) does he smile . . . smiles

5. It's raining. People who usually ____ their bicycles ____ them today.
   (A) ride . . . are riding
   (B) riding . . . ride
   (C) ride . . . aren't riding
   (D) don't ride . . . don't ride

6. I usually go to the doctor when I'm ____.
   (A) happy
   (B) hungry
   (C) sick
   (D) angry

7. I'm ____ because I'm tired.
   (A) biting my nails
   (B) yawning
   (C) smiling
   (D) perspiring

8. She's walking to school today because her ____ is broken.
   (A) computer
   (B) sink
   (C) lamp
   (D) bicycle

9. The receptionist at our office ____ the telephone.
   (A) types
   (B) answers
   (C) rushes
   (D) takes

10. I'm a police officer. Every morning I ____ on Main Street.
   (A) deliver
   (B) walk
   (C) direct traffic
   (D) make

SKILLS CHECK 

Match the "can do" statement and the correct sentence.

____ 1. I can describe my feelings and emotions.
____ 2. I can describe how I react to things.
____ 3. I can ask about a person's activity.
____ 4. I can express surprise.
____ 5. I can describe a repair problem.
____ 6. I can react to bad news.
____ 7. I can describe people's work.

a. My sink is broken.
b. What are you doing?
c. Mail carriers deliver mail.
d. I'm happy.
e. I'm sorry to hear that.
f. That's strange!
g. When I'm nervous, I perspire.

Choose the correct answer.

1. I ____, but I ____.
- (A) can't ski . . . can't skate
- (B) can ski . . . can't skate
- (C) can ski . . . can skate
- (D) can't ski . . . can ski

2. Carlos is busy today. He ____ fix his car.
- (A) has to
- (B) has
- (C) have
- (D) have to

3. Please fill out this form in duplicate. You ____ use a pencil. You ____ use a pen.
- (A) can . . . have to
- (B) have to . . . have to
- (C) can't . . . have to
- (D) have to . . . can

4. Roberta is a very bad singer. She ____ sing very well.
- (A) can
- (B) has to
- (C) can't
- (D) doesn't have to

5. A. Can Timothy repair cars?
B. No, he ____, but he ____ repair bicycles.
- (A) can . . . can't
- (B) can't . . . can't
- (C) has to . . . can
- (D) can't . . . can

6. Ramon can ____. He's looking for a job as a secretary.
- (A) bake
- (B) paint
- (C) type
- (D) ski

7. Ann can ____. She's looking for a job as a mechanic.
- (A) repair cars
- (B) fix stoves
- (C) skate
- (D) paint pictures

8. Ivan can ____. He's looking for a job as a salesperson.
- (A) file
- (B) operate equipment
- (C) use tools
- (D) take inventory

9. I'm a construction worker. I can ____.
- (A) use business software
- (B) build things
- (C) take inventory
- (D) use a cash register

10. I'm sick. I can't go to work today. I have to ____.
- (A) visit my friends
- (B) do my exercises
- (C) go to the doctor
- (D) wash my car

SKILLS CHECK 

Match the "can do" statement and the correct sentence.

____	**1.** I can tell my occupation.	**a.**	I can drive a truck.
____	**2.** I can ask about a person's skills.	**b.**	I'm looking for a job as a baker.
____	**3.** I can tell about my skills.	**c.**	He's annoyed.
____	**4.** I can express my job interests.	**d.**	I'm a mechanic.
____	**5.** I can express inability to do something.	**e.**	I have to do my homework.
____	**6.** I can express obligation.	**f.**	I'm sorry.
____	**7.** I can describe a person's emotions.	**g.**	Can you use a cash register?
____	**8.** I can apologize.	**h.**	I can't go to a movie.

Choose the correct answer.

1. I'm looking forward to this weekend. We're _____ a concert.
   - (A) going
   - (B) going to go
   - (C) going to go to
   - (D) go to
2. A. What's the forecast?
   B. According to the newspaper, _____ tomorrow.
   - (A) it rains
   - (B) it's going be sunny
   - (C) it's be foggy
   - (D) it's going to rain
3. _____ the train leave?
   - (A) When
   - (B) What time
   - (C) What time does
   - (D) When is the time when
4. The bus leaves _____.
   - (A) ten forty-five
   - (B) at nine fifteen
   - (C) noon
   - (D) in a quarter to five
5. I _____ see a movie, but my friend _____ go to the park.
   - (A) want . . . want
   - (B) want . . . wants
   - (C) want to . . . want to
   - (D) want to . . . wants to
6. June is my favorite _____.
   - (A) week of the year
   - (B) day of the week
   - (C) month of the year
   - (D) holiday
7. We're going to the beach tomorrow. It's going to _____.
   - (A) rain
   - (B) snow
   - (C) be cold and cloudy
   - (D) be warm and sunny
8. My sister and I are going to a baseball game at two o'clock _____.
   - (A) tomorrow afternoon
   - (B) this morning
   - (C) this evening
   - (D) tonight
9. I'm going to save a lot of money because I want to _____.
   - (A) go to the library
   - (B) see a movie
   - (C) buy a car
   - (D) have a picnic
10. We're having breakfast now. We're going to have lunch _____.
    - (A) at noon
    - (B) at midnight
    - (C) tonight
    - (D) tomorrow morning

SKILLS CHECK

Match the "can do" statement and the correct sentence.

_____ 1. I can give the time.
_____ 2. I can say the months of the year.
_____ 3. I can name the seasons.
_____ 4. I can ask about future plans.
_____ 5. I can tell about future plans.
_____ 6. I can ask about the weather.
_____ 7. I can ask the time.
_____ 8. I can tell about future weather.

a. Spring, summer, winter, fall.
b. What are you going to do tomorrow?
c. It's going to be sunny.
d. I'm going to go swimming.
e. What time is it?
f. It's two o'clock.
g. What's the forecast?
h. January, February, March, . . .

Choose the correct answer.

1. ____ all morning today, and now I have a headache.
   - (A) I study
   - (B) I studied
   - (C) I'm going to study
   - (D) I'm studying

2. David ____ TV today. ____ every day.
   - (A) watches . . . He watches
   - (B) watch . . . He's going to watch
   - (C) watched . . . He watches
   - (D) watched . . . He's watching

3. ____ yesterday, and ____ tomorrow.
   - (A) I'm going to clean . . . I cleaned
   - (B) I cleaned . . . I'm going to clean
   - (C) I clean . . . I'm going to clean
   - (D) I'm cleaning . . . I'm cleaning

4. I ____ for the bus all morning.
   - (A) waited
   - (B) rode
   - (C) finished
   - (D) wanted

5. I ____ all afternoon, and now I have a terrible backache.
   - (A) sang
   - (B) talked
   - (C) rested
   - (D) sat

6. Amanda ____ her broken front steps.
   - (A) worked
   - (B) fixed
   - (C) served
   - (D) asked

7. Henry ate cookies all day, and now he has ____.
   - (A) a fever
   - (B) an earache
   - (C) a cold
   - (D) a stomachache

8. I ____ at work at 9:00 this morning.
   - (A) arrived
   - (B) showed
   - (C) rode
   - (D) turned

9. My son ____ his homework at 8:30.
   - (A) looked
   - (B) stayed
   - (C) finished
   - (D) watched

10. We ____ a video of our trip to Japan.
    - (A) asked
    - (B) showed
    - (C) sang
    - (D) rested

SKILLS CHECK 

Match the "can do" statement and the correct sentence.

____	1. I can describe ailments.	a.	I'm sorry to hear that.
____	2. I can ask about a person's health.	b.	I feel terrible.
____	3. I can express sympathy.	c.	Hello. This is Bob Wilson.
____	4. I can say that I feel well.	d.	What did you do yesterday?
____	5. I can say that I don't feel well.	e.	How do you feel today?
____	6. I can ask about past activities.	f.	I worked all day yesterday.
____	7. I can tell about past activities.	g.	I feel fine.
____	8. I can call someone.	h.	I have a headache.

Choose the correct answer.

1. ____ the news this morning?
   Ⓐ You listen to
   Ⓑ Did you listened to
   Ⓒ Did you listen to
   Ⓓ Listened you to

2. ____ yesterday evening?
   Ⓐ What you did
   Ⓑ What did you do
   Ⓒ What did you did
   Ⓓ What did you

3. A. Did you see your friends yesterday?
   B. ____
   Ⓐ Yes, they did.
   Ⓑ Yes, did I.
   Ⓒ Yes, I did.
   Ⓓ No, I did.

4. A. Did Maria take the bus today?
   B. No, ____. She ____ the train.
   Ⓐ she didn't . . . took
   Ⓑ she did . . . took
   Ⓒ didn't she . . . didn't take
   Ⓓ she didn't . . . didn't take

5. I ____ to the park. I ____ to the bank.
   Ⓐ didn't went . . . went
   Ⓑ not went . . . did go
   Ⓒ went not . . . did went
   Ⓓ didn't go . . . went

6. Susan arrived late for work because she missed the ____.
   Ⓐ apartment
   Ⓑ office
   Ⓒ bus
   Ⓓ newspaper

7. I met a ____ on the way to work today.
   Ⓐ book
   Ⓑ friend
   Ⓒ bank
   Ⓓ car

8. After he ____ the train, Omar walked to the office.
   Ⓐ got off
   Ⓑ got up
   Ⓒ had
   Ⓓ went

9. I ____ my house at 7:45 to go to school.
   Ⓐ arrived
   Ⓑ took
   Ⓒ saw
   Ⓓ left

10. After work today, I ____ some groceries.
   Ⓐ ate
   Ⓑ had
   Ⓒ bought
   Ⓓ made

SKILLS CHECK 

Match the "can do" statement and the correct sentence.

____ 1. I can ask about past activities.
____ 2. I can tell about past activities.
____ 3. I can apologize for something.
____ 4. I can tell about obligation.
____ 5. I can give an excuse for lateness.
____ 6. I can describe ailments.

a. I had to go to the dentist.
b. I'm sorry I'm late.
c. We went to the supermarket.
d. I had a stomachache.
e. What did you do yesterday?
f. I missed the bus.

CHAPTER 17 • Check-up Test • Skills Check

Choose the correct answer.

1. She ___ upset, and her parents ___ upset, too.
Ⓐ was . . . was
Ⓑ were . . . was
Ⓒ was . . . were
Ⓓ were . . . were

2. Before we bought an air conditioner, our apartment ___ always hot. Now our apartment ___ very comfortable.
Ⓐ is . . . is
Ⓑ is . . . was
Ⓒ was . . . is
Ⓓ was . . . was

3. Carlos ___ at work yesterday. He stayed home because he ___ sick.
Ⓐ was . . . was
Ⓑ wasn't . . . was
Ⓒ wasn't . . . wasn't
Ⓓ was . . . wasn't

4. My wife and I ___ late for the plane. We ___ early.
Ⓐ wasn't . . . was
Ⓑ weren't . . . were
Ⓒ were . . . were
Ⓓ weren't . . . weren't

5. I ___ sleep well because I ___ tired.
Ⓐ wasn't . . . wasn't
Ⓑ didn't . . . weren't
Ⓒ didn't . . . was
Ⓓ didn't . . . wasn't

6. I ate a big breakfast today because I was very ___.
Ⓐ dull
Ⓑ full
Ⓒ hungry
Ⓓ shiny

7. We didn't like the restaurant because the food ___.
Ⓐ was bad
Ⓑ was sad
Ⓒ wasn't bad
Ⓓ was quiet

8. My best friend moved to South America. I really ___ her.
Ⓐ look forward to
Ⓑ meet
Ⓒ miss
Ⓓ see

9. I usually ___ with my friends over the Internet.
Ⓐ grow up
Ⓑ go
Ⓒ see
Ⓓ communicate

10. We cleaned our living room windows because ___.
Ⓐ they were enormous
Ⓑ they were dirty
Ⓒ they weren't dirty
Ⓓ they were clean

SKILLS CHECK

Match the "can do" statement and the correct sentence.

___ **1.** I can describe my feelings and emotions.
___ **2.** I can describe my health.
___ **3.** I can describe an object.
___ **4.** I can ask for a recommendation.
___ **5.** I can give a recommendation.
___ **6.** I can ask about past activities.
___ **7.** I can ask about the weather.

a. I recommend *Presto* Toothpaste.
b. Can you recommend a good soap?
c. I was sick.
d. Was it cold yesterday?
e. My armchair was uncomfortable.
f. I was sad.
g. Did you go to the doctor yesterday?

APPENDIX

Student Book Listening Scripts

Chapter 9 – Page 84

Listen and choose the correct answer.

1. My brother lives in Chicago.
2. My name is Peter. I work in an office.
3. This is my friend Carla. She speaks Italian.
4. My sister drives a bus in Chicago.
5. We read the newspaper every day.
6. My parents visit their friends every weekend.
7. Charlie cooks in a Greek restaurant.
8. My brother and I paint houses.
9. My friend Betty calls me every day.
10. My parents usually shop at the mall.

Chapter 10 – Page 93

WHAT'S THE WORD?

Listen and choose the word you hear.

1. Do you work on Monday?
2. Does your daughter go to this school?
3. We do a different activity every Sunday.
4. Larry doesn't play a sport.
5. We don't go to Stanley's Restaurant.
6. Sally goes to a health club every week.
7. She baby-sits for her neighbors every Thursday.
8. They go to work every morning.

WHAT'S THE ANSWER?

Listen and choose the correct response.

1. Do you speak Korean?
2. Does Mrs. Wilson go to Stanley's Restaurant?
3. Does your sister live in Los Angeles?
4. Do you and your brother clean the house together?
5. Does your husband like American food?
6. Do you go to school on the weekend?
7. Do you and your friends play tennis?
8. Does your cousin live in this neighborhood?

Side by Side Gazette – Page 98

You're calling the International Cafe! Listen to the recorded announcement. Match the day of the week and the kind of entertainment.

Hello! This is the International Cafe—your special place for wonderful entertainment every day of the week! Every day the International Cafe presents a different kind of entertainment. On Monday, Antonio Bello plays Italian classical music. On Tuesday, Miguel Garcia reads Spanish poetry. On Wednesday, Amanda Silva sings Brazilian jazz. On Thursday, Nina Markova reads Russian short stories. On Friday, Hiroshi Tanaka plays Japanese rock music. On Saturday, Rita Rivera sings Mexican popular music. And on Sunday, Slim Wilkins sings American country music. So come to the International Cafe—your special place for wonderful entertainment . . . every day of the week!

Chapter 11 – Page 105

Listen to the conversations. Who and what are they talking about?

1. A. How often do you visit him?
   B. I visit him every week.
2. A. How often do you wash them?
   B. I wash them every year.
3. A. Do you write to her very often?
   B. I write to her every month.
4. A. Is it broken?
   B. Yes. I'm fixing it now.
5. A. How often do you see them?
   B. I see them every day.
6. A. How often do you use it?
   B. I use it all the time.
7. A. When does he wash it?
   B. He washes it every Sunday.
8. A. Do you see him very often?
   B. No. I rarely see him.
9. A. Do you study with them very often?
   B. Yes. I study with them all the time.

Chapter 12 – Page 112

Listen and choose the correct answer.

1. What are you doing?
2. What does the office assistant do?
3. What's the receptionist doing?
4. Is he tired?
5. What do you do when you're scared?
6. Where do you usually study?

Side by Side Gazette – Page 115

Listen to these news reports. Match the news and the city.

A. You're listening to WBOS in Boston. And now here's Randy Ryan with today's news.
B. Good morning. Well, the people in Boston who usually take the subway to work aren't taking it today. There's a big problem with the subway system in Boston.

A. You're listening to KSAC in Sacramento. And now here's Jessica Chen with the morning news.
B. Good morning. The big news here in Sacramento is the traffic! Sacramento police officers are on strike today, and nobody is directing traffic. There are traffic problems all around the city!

(continued)

A. This is WCHI in Chicago. And now here's Mike Maxwell with today's news.

B. Good morning. It's snowing very hard in Chicago right now. As a result, the streets of the city are empty. People aren't walking or driving to work. There aren't any trucks or buses on the street. And mail carriers aren't delivering the mail.

A. You're listening to CTOR in Toronto. And now here's Mark Mitchell with today's news.

B. It's a quiet Tuesday morning in Toronto. There aren't any bad traffic problems right now, and there aren't any problems with the subway system or the buses.

A. You're listening to WMIA in Miami. And now here's today's news.

B. Good morning. This is Rita Rodriguez with the news. The children of Miami who usually take school buses to school aren't taking them this morning. The men and women who drive the school buses are on strike. Some children are walking to school today. Many students are staying home.

Chapter 13 – Page 121

Can or Can't?

Listen and choose the word you hear.

1. I can speak Spanish.
2. He can't paint.
3. She can type.
4. We can't build things.
5. They can use tools.
6. We can't operate equipment.

What Can They Do?

Listen and choose what each person can do.

1. He can't file. He can type.
2. They can cook. They can't bake.
3. She can repair locks. She can't repair stoves.
4. I can't drive a truck. I can drive a bus.
5. He can teach French. He can't teach English.
6. We can take inventory. We can't paint.

Chapter 14 – Page 132

Listen and choose the words you hear.

1. A. When are you going to buy a computer?
   B. Tomorrow.
2. A. When are your neighbors going to move?
   B. Next November.
3. A. When are you going to visit me?
   B. Next month.
4. A. When are you going to do your laundry?
   B. This evening.
5. A. When are you going to begin your vacation?
   B. This Sunday.
6. A. When are we going to go to the concert?
   B. This Thursday.
7. A. When are you going to wash the windows?
   B. This afternoon.
8. A. When is she going to get her driver's license?
   B. Next week.
9. A. When is your daughter going to finish college?
   B. Next winter.
10. A. When is the landlord going to fix the kitchen sink?
    B. At once.

Side by Side Gazette – Page 140

Listen and match the theaters and the movies.

Thank you for calling the Multiplex Cinema! The Multiplex Cinema has five theaters with the best movies in town!

Now showing in Theater One: *The Spanish Dancer,* a film from Spain about the life of the famous dancer Carlos Montero. Show times are at one fifteen, three thirty, and seven o'clock.

Now showing in Theater Two: *When Are You Going to Call the Plumber?*, starring Julie Richards and Harry Grant. In this comedy, a husband and wife have a lot of problems in their new house. Show times are at two thirty, four forty-five, and seven fifteen.

Now showing in Theater Three: *The Fortune Teller*. In this film from Brazil, a woman tells people all the things that are going to happen in their lives. Show times are at five o'clock, seven forty-five, and ten fifteen.

Now showing in Theater Four: *The Time Zone Machine*, the exciting new science fiction movie. Professor Stanley Carrington's new machine can send people to different time zones around the world. Show times are at five fifteen, eight o'clock, and ten thirty. There's also a special show at midnight.

Now showing in Theater Five: *Tomorrow Is Right Now*. In this new drama, a truck driver from Australia falls in love with a businesswoman from Paris. Where are they going to live, and what are they going to tell their friends? See it and find out! Show times are at six o'clock, eight thirty, and ten forty-five.

The Multiplex Cinema is on Harrison Avenue, across from the shopping mall. So come and see a movie at the Multiplex Cinema. You're going to have a good time! Thank you, and have a nice day!

Chapter 15 – Page 147

Listen and choose the word you hear.

1. We plant flowers in our garden in the spring.
2. I worked at the office all day.
3. They studied English all morning.
4. Mr. and Mrs. Jones sit in their living room all day.
5. They drank lemonade all summer.
6. I waited for the bus all morning.
7. They finish their work at five o'clock.

8. We invited our friends to the party.
9. I eat cheese and crackers.
10. She cleaned her apartment all afternoon.
11. We wash our clothes at the laundromat.
12. He watched TV all evening.

Chapter 16 – Page 155

Listen and put a check next to all the things these people did today.

Carla got up early this morning. She took a shower, she had breakfast, and she took the subway to work. She didn't have lunch today. She left work at five thirty, and she met her mother at six o'clock. They had dinner at a restaurant. Then they saw a movie.

Brian had a busy day today. This morning he fixed his car. Then he cleaned his yard. This afternoon he planted flowers, and then he washed his windows. This evening he read the newspaper, and he wrote to his brother. Then he took a bath.

Chapter 17 – Page 163

Listen and choose the correct answer.

1. Before we bought Captain Crispy Cereal, we were always sick. Now we're always healthy.
2. We bought new chairs for our living room because our old chairs were very uncomfortable. We love our new chairs. They're VERY comfortable.
3. My daughter Lucy didn't finish her milk this morning. She wasn't very thirsty.
4. Fred was very upset this morning. He was late for the bus, and he didn't get to work on time.
5. Hmm. Where are Peter and Mary? They were at work yesterday, but they aren't here today.
6. Our kitchen floor was very dull. Our neighbors recommended Sparkle Floor Wax, and now our kitchen floor isn't dull any more. It's shiny!

Side by Side Gazette – Page 165

Listen and match the products.

ANNOUNCER: And now a word from our sponsors.
WOMAN: I had a problem with my teeth. They were very yellow, and I was upset. I went to my dentist, and she recommended Dazzle. So I went to the store and I bought some. Now I brush my teeth with Dazzle every day. My teeth aren't yellow any more. They're white. They're VERY white! Thank you, Dazzle!
ANNOUNCER: Are YOUR teeth yellow? Try Dazzle today!

TED: Bob! This kitchen floor is beautiful!
BOB: Thanks, Ted.
TED: Is it new?
BOB: Oh, no! This is my old kitchen floor.
TED: But it's so shiny!
BOB: That's right, Ted. It IS shiny, because I bought Shiny-Time!
TED: Shiny-Time?
BOB: Yes. Shiny-Time!
ANNOUNCER: That's right, Ted. YOU can have a shiny kitchen floor, too. Use Shiny-Time . . . every time!

WOMAN: Alan? What's the matter?
MAN: I don't know. I jog all the time, but today I'm really tired. Tell me, Julie, you're NEVER tired. You're always energetic. How do you do it?
WOMAN: Energy Plus!
MAN: Energy Plus?
WOMAN: Yes, Alan, Energy Plus! Before I bought Energy Plus, I was always tired like you. But now I'm energetic all the time!
ANNOUNCER: Tired? Try Energy Plus today! You can find it in supermarkets and drug stores everywhere.

PRESIDENT: Thank you. Thank you very much.
ASSISTANT: That was excellent, Mr. President.
PRESIDENT: Thank you, Ron. You know, I have a terrible sore throat.
ASSISTANT: I can hear that, Mr. President. Here. Try one of these.
PRESIDENT: What are they?
ASSISTANT: Lucky Lemon Drops.
PRESIDENT: Lucky Lemon Drops?
ASSISTANT: Yes, Mr. President. They're really good for a sore throat.
PRESIDENT: Thanks, Ron.
ANNOUNCER: Lucky Lemon Drops. They're good for the president! They're good for you!

WOMAN: My dog's fur was dull. It was VERY dull, and my dog was very sad. Then I bought K-9 Shine! Yes, K-9 Shine. I washed my dog with K-9 Shine, and now his fur is shiny! It's very shiny, and my dog is very happy!
ANNOUNCER: Try K-9 Shine today! YOUR dog's fur can be shiny, too!

Activity Workbook Listening Scripts

Page 63 Exercise B

Listen and choose the correct response.

1. What's your name?
2. What language do you speak?
3. What do they do every day?
4. Where do you live?
5. What language do you speak?
6. What do you do every day?

Page 66 Exercise G

Listen and circle the word you hear.

1. We live in Paris.
2. Where do you live?
3. What language does he speak?
4. Every day I listen to Greek music.
5. Every day she watches English TV shows.
6. What do they eat every day?
7. Every day I sing Korean songs.
8. Every day she eats Chinese food.
9. Every day he reads Mexican newspapers.

Page 70 Exercise D

Listen and choose the correct response.

1. What kind of food do you like?
2. Do they paint houses?
3. Why does he go to that restaurant?
4. When does Mrs. Miller cook dinner?
5. Do you work in a bank?
6. Where do they live?
7. What do your children do in the park?
8. Does your friend Patty drive a taxi?
9. Why do they shop in that store?

Page 72 Exercise I

Listen and choose the correct response.

1. Do you do a different kind of sport every day?
2. Does Bob write for the school newspaper?
3. Do Mr. and Mrs. Chang live near a bus stop?
4. Does your sister baby-sit every weekend?
5. Does Timmy do a different activity every day?
6. Do your children play in the orchestra?
7. Does your son sing in the choir?
8. Do your parents go to the park every day?
9. Do you play cards with your friends?

Page 75 Exercise D

Listen and choose the correct response.

Ex. What do Patty and Peter do during the week?

1. When do you watch your favorite TV program?
2. Why do you eat Italian food?
3. Does Carlos visit his grandparents in Puerto Rico?
4. What kind of books do you like?
5. Where do your nephews live?

Page 77 Exercise C

Listen and put a check under the correct picture.

1. How often do you read them?
2. I call her every day.
3. I don't like him.
4. I wash it every weekend.
5. He calls us all the time.
6. I say "hello" to them every morning.

Page 78 Exercise G

Listen and choose the correct answer.

1. Henry's car is always very dirty.
2. My husband sometimes makes dinner.
3. My neighbors play loud music at night.
4. My grandparents rarely speak English.
5. Jane always spends a lot of time with her friends.
6. I rarely study in the library.

Page 82 Exercise N

Listen and choose the correct response.

1. Do you have curly hair?
2. Are you married?
3. Does he have brown eyes?
4. Do you have a brother?
5. Do you usually go out on weekends?
6. Is your husband heavy?
7. Do you live in the city?
8. Do you have short hair?

Page 89 Exercise H

As you listen to each story, read the sentences and check yes or no.

Jennifer and Jason

Jennifer and Jason are visiting their grandfather in California. They're sad today. Their grandfather usually takes them to the park, but he isn't taking them to the park today.

Our Boss

Our boss usually smiles at the office, but he isn't smiling today. He's upset because the people in our office aren't working very hard today. It's Friday, and everybody is thinking about the weekend.

On Vacation

When my family and I are on vacation, I always have a good time. I usually play tennis, but when it's cold, I play games on my computer and watch videos. Today is a beautiful day, and I'm swimming at the beach.

Timmy and His Brother

Timmy and his brother are watching a science fiction movie. Timmy is covering his eyes because he's scared. He doesn't like science fiction movies. Timmy's brother isn't scared. He likes science fiction movies.

Page 91 Exercise E

Listen and choose the correct response.

Ex. What are Peter and Tom doing today?

1. What do mail carriers do every day?
2. Where are you going today?
3. What do you do when you're scared?
4. Do you usually use a typewriter?
5. Where do you usually study?

Page 93 Exercise D

Listen and circle the word you hear.

1. Our teacher can speak French.
2. I can't play the piano.
3. He can paint houses.
4. My sister can play soccer.
5. They can't sing.
6. Can you drive a bus?
7. I can't read Japanese newspapers.
8. My son Tommy can play the drums.
9. Their children can't swim.
10. Can your husband cook?
11. We can't skate.
12. I can use a cash register.

Page 97 Exercise K

Listen and circle the words you hear.

1. We have to go to the supermarket.
2. My son has to play his violin every day.
3. We can use business software on our computers.
4. Boris has to speak English every day now.
5. I can't cook Italian food.
6. Apartment building superintendents have to repair locks and paint apartments.
7. That actress can't act!
8. Our children have to use a computer to do their homework.
9. Mr. Johnson can operate equipment.

Page 98 Exercise M

Listen and choose the correct answer.

1. I'm sorry. I can't go to the movies with you today. I have to go to the dentist.
2. I can't go to the party on Saturday. I have to wash my clothes.
3. I can't have lunch with you, but I can have dinner.
4. We can't go skiing this weekend. We have to paint our kitchen.
5. I'm very busy today. I have to go shopping, and I have to cook dinner for my family.
6. I can't see a play with you on Friday because I have to baby-sit. But I can see a play with you on Saturday.

Page 102 Exercise H

Listen and circle the words you hear.

1. I'm going to visit her this year.
2. I'm going to write to my uncle right away.
3. I'm going to call them this Monday.
4. When are you going to cut your hair?
5. I'm going to fix it next Tuesday.
6. We're going to see them this December.
7. They're going to visit us this winter.
8. I'm going to clean it at once.
9. We're going to spend time with them this August.
10. I'm going to wash them immediately.
11. You're going to see us next week.
12. When are you going to call the plumber?

Page 103 Exercise J

Listen to the following weather forecasts and circle the correct answers.

Today's Weather Forecast

This is Mike Martinez with today's weather forecast. This afternoon it's going to be cool and cloudy, with temperatures from 50 to 55 degrees Fahrenheit. This evening it's going to be foggy and warm, but it isn't going to rain.

This Weekend's Weather Forecast

This is Barbara Burrows with your weekend weather forecast. Tonight it's going to be clear and warm, with 60 degree temperatures. On Saturday you can swim at the beach. It's going to be sunny and very hot, with temperatures between 90 and 95 degrees Fahrenheit. But take your umbrella with you on Sunday because it's going to be cool and it's going to rain.

Monday's Weather Forecast

This is Al Alberts with Monday's weather forecast. Monday morning it's going to be cool and nice, but Monday afternoon wear your gloves and your boots because it's going to be very cold and it's going to snow! On Tuesday morning the skiing is going to be wonderful because it's going to be sunny and very warm!

Page 108 Exercise T

Listen and write the time you hear.

1. It's seven forty-five.
2. It's six fifteen.
3. It's four thirty.
4. It's nine fifteen.
5. It's midnight.
6. It's five o'clock.
7. It's a quarter to nine.
8. It's a quarter after eight.
9. It's one forty-five.
10. It's noon.
11. It's eleven thirty.
12. It's a quarter to three.

Page 113 Exercise G

Listen to the story. Fill in the correct times.

Every day at school I study English, science, mathematics, music, and Chinese. English class begins at 8:30. I go to science at 10:15 and mathematics at 11:00. We have lunch at 12:15. We go to music at 12:45, and we have Chinese at 1:30.

Page 114 Exercise B

Listen to the story. Put the number under the correct picture.

Everybody in my family is sick today.

My parents are sick.

1. My father has a stomachache.
2. My mother has a backache.

My brother and my sister are sick, too.

3. My sister Alice has an earache.
4. My brother David has a toothache.

My grandparents are also sick.

5. My grandmother has a cold.
6. My grandfather has a sore throat.
7. Even my dog is sick! He has a fever!

Yes, everybody in my family is sick today . . . everybody except me!

How do I feel today?

8. I feel fine!

Page 117 Exercise F

Listen and circle the correct answer.

Example 1: I study.
Example 2: I played cards.

1. I planted flowers.
2. I shave.
3. I cried.
4. I typed.
5. I work.
6. I shouted.
7. I clean.
8. I studied.
9. I fixed my car.
10. I paint.
11. I smile.
12. I cooked.

Page 126 Exercise I

Listen and choose the correct response.

1. When did you write to your girlfriend?
2. When does your neighbor wash his car?
3. Who did your parents visit?
4. Where does Irene do yoga?
5. When did your son go to sleep?
6. When do you clean your apartment?
7. Where did you take your grandchildren?
8. What did you make for dinner?
9. When does Carla read her e-mail?
10. When did you get up today?

Page 129 Exercise B

Listen and circle the word you hear.

1. My husband is thin.
2. She was very hungry.
3. They were tired today.
4. He was very energetic at school today.
5. My wife is at the clinic.
6. Their clothes were clean.
7. My children are very sick today.
8. My parents are home tonight.
9. He was very full this morning.
10. The Lopez family is on vacation.
11. Their neighbors are very noisy.
12. These clothes were dirty.

Page 131 Exercise E

Listen and circle the word you hear.

1. I wasn't busy yesterday.
2. We were at the movies last night.
3. They weren't home today.
4. Tom was on time for his plane.
5. It wasn't cold yesterday.
6. They weren't at the baseball game.
7. My friends were late for the party.
8. The doctor was in her office at noon.

Page 134 Exercise I

Listen and choose the correct response.

1. Where were you born?
2. Where did you grow up?
3. What was your favorite subject in school?
4. When did you move here?
5. What did you look like when you were young?
6. Did you have freckles?
7. What do you do in your spare time?
8. Did you have a favorite hero?

Page 137 Exercise F

Listen and circle the word you hear.

Ex. Is Jane rich or poor?

1. It was a nice day today.
2. My friends were thirsty at lunch.
3. Who is your favorite hero?
4. Were Mr. and Mrs. Parker at home last weekend?
5. My new couch is uncomfortable.
6. My cousins were late for their plane.
7. Before I met Howard, I was very sad.
8. Your children are very cute.

Student Book Thematic Glossary

Ailments 141

backache
cold
cough
earache
fever
headache
sore throat
stomachache
toothache

Days of the Week 87

Sunday
Monday
Tuesday
Wednesday
Thursday
Friday
Saturday

Describing Feelings and Emotions

annoyed **124**
depressed **122**
embarrassed **107**
hungry **107**
nervous **107**
scared **107**
sick **107**
thirsty **107**

Describing People and Things

active **90**
athletic **90**
bad **112**
blond **102**
closed **165**
comfortable **157**
cute **163**
dark **165**
dry **165**
dull **157**
energetic **112**
enormous **157**
exciting **162**
fancy **165**
fast **165**
full **157**
healthy **157**
high **165**
late **161**
light **165**
long **165**
low **165**
messy **165**
neat **165**
open **165**
outgoing **94**
plain **165**
popular **94**
shiny **157**
shy **94**
slow **165**
tiny **157**
uncomfortable **157**
wet **165**

Everyday Activities

baby-sit **87**
call **79**
comb *my* hair **97**
deliver **113**
do *yoga* **87**
drive **79**
get dressed **97**
get up **97**
go **89**
go *dancing* **87**
go to bed **97**
go to school **97**
go to work **97**
jog **87**
see **87**
sell **79**
shave **135**
skate **118**
ski **118**
speak **79**
sweep **111**
take a bath **97**
take a shower **97**
take a taxi **115**
take the bus **113**
take the subway **115**
take the train **115**
type **112**
visit **79**
walk **111**
work **79**

Months of the Year 127

January
February
March
April
May
June
July
August
September
October
November
December

Occupations

architect **139**
baker **117**
carpenter **139**
cashier **139**
chef **117**
construction worker **117**
custodian **112**
dancer **117**
farmer **139**
journalist **103**
lawyer **139**
mail carrier **113**
mechanic **117**
office assistant **112**
painter **139**
pilot **139**
police officer **113**
receptionist **112**
salesperson **117**
secretary **117**
singer **117**
translator **139**
truck driver **117**
waiter **139**
waitress **139**

Seasons 127

spring
summer
fall/autumn
winter

Skills

build **115**
file **120**
operate **120**
repair **120**
sort *the mail* **112**
speak *Spanish* **79**
take inventory **120**
type **112**
use **111**

Time Expressions

afternoon **92**
evening **92**
month **99**
morning **92**
week **92**
weekend **83**

Cardinal Numbers

1	one	20	twenty
2	two	21	twenty-one
3	three	22	twenty-two
4	four	.	.
5	five	.	.
6	six	29	twenty-nine
7	seven	30	thirty
8	eight	40	forty
9	nine	50	fifty
10	ten	60	sixty
11	eleven	70	seventy
12	twelve	80	eighty
13	thirteen	90	ninety
14	fourteen	100	one hundred
15	fifteen	200	two hundred
16	sixteen	300	three hundred
17	seventeen	.	.
18	eighteen	.	.
19	nineteen	900	nine hundred
		1,000	one thousand
		2,000	two thousand
		3,000	three thousand
		.	.
		10,000	ten thousand
		100,000	one hundred thousand
		1,000,000	one million

Irregular Verbs: Past Tense

be	was
begin	began
buy	bought
do	did
drink	drank
drive	drove
eat	ate
forget	forgot
get	got
go	went
grow	grew
have	had
make	made
meet	met
read	read
ride	rode
see	saw
sing	sang
sit	sat
steal	stole
take	took
write	wrote

Index

Correlation Key

Student Book Pages	Activity Workbook Pages
Chapter 9	
80	62–63 Exercises A, B
81	63 Exercise C–66
82	67–68
Chapter 10	
88	69
89	70–71
90–91	72–73
95	74
Check-Up Test	75
Gazette	75a–b
Chapter 11	
100	76–77
101	78–79
102	80
103	81–82
Chapter 12	
108–109	83–86
110–111	87–90
Check-Up Test	91
Gazette	91a–b
Chapter 13	
118	92–93 Exercise B
119	93 Exercise C–95
122	96–97
123	98–99

Student Book Pages	Activity Workbook Pages
Chapter 14	
128	100
129	101
130–131	102–103 Exercise I
133	103 Exercise J–107
134–135	108–111
Check-Up Test	112–113
Gazette	113a–b
Chapter 15	
142	114–115
143	116–117
144–145	118–121
Chapter 16	
150	122–123
151	124–125
152	126
153	127–128
Chapter 17	
158	129
159	130
160	131
161	132–133
163	134–135
Check-Up Test	136–137
Gazette	137a–b

SIDE *by* SIDE *Extra* Activity Workbook Audio Program

The *Side by Side Extra* Activity Workbook Digital Audio CDs contain all Workbook listening activities and GrammarRaps and GrammarSongs for entertaining language practice through rhythm and music. Students can use the Audio Program to extend their language learning through self-study outside the classroom. The Digital Audio CDs also include MP3 files of the audio program for downloading to a computer or audio player.

Audio Program Contents

Track	Page	Activity
CD 1		
1		Introduction
Chapter 9		
2	p. 63	Exercise B Listening
3	p. 65	Exercise E GrammarRap
4	p. 66	Exercise G Listening
5	p. 68	Exercise J Listen and Pronounce
Chapter 10		
6	p. 70	Exercise D Listening
7	p. 72	Exercise I Listening
8	p. 73	Exercise J GrammarRap
Check-Up Test: Chapters 9–10		
9	p. 75	Exercise D Listening
Chapter 11		
10	p. 77	Exercise C Listening
11	p. 78	Exercise G Listening
12	p. 79	Exercise I GrammarRap
13	p. 82	Exercise N Listening
Chapter 12		
14	p. 85	Exercise C GrammarRap
15	p. 85	Exercise D GrammarRap
16	p. 89	Exercise H Listening
Check-Up Test: Chapters 11–12		
17	p. 91	Exercise E Listening

Track	Page	Activity
CD 2		
1		Introduction
Chapter 13		
2	p. 93	Exercise D Listening
3	p. 95	Exercise G GrammarRap
4	p. 97	Exercise K Listening
5	p. 98	Exercise M Listening
6	p. 99	Exercise N GrammarRap
7	p. 99	Exercise O GrammarRap
Chapter 14		
8	p. 101	Exercise D GrammarRap
9	p. 102	Exercise H Listening
10	p. 103	Exercise J Listening
11	p. 107	Exercise Q GrammarRap
12	p. 108	Exercise T Listening
13	p. 110	Exercise W GrammarRap
14	p. 111	Exercise X GrammarSong
Check-Up Test: Chapters 13–14		
15	p. 113	Exercise G Listening
Chapter 15		
16	p. 114	Exercise B Listening
17	p. 115	Exercise C GrammarRap
18	p. 117	Exercise F Listening
19	p. 120	Exercise J GrammarRap
Chapter 16		
20	p. 125	Exercise F GrammarRap Rhyming Game
21	p. 126	Exercise I Listening
22	p. 128	Exercise L GrammarRap
23	p. 128	Exercise M GrammarRap
Chapter 17		
24	p. 129	Exercise B Listening
25	p. 131	Exercise E Listening
26	p. 133	Exercise G Grammar Rap
27	p. 134	Exercise I Listening
28	p. 135	Exercise J GrammarRap
Check-Up Test: Chapters 15–17		
29	p. 137	Exercise F Listening